# Ninja Dual Zone Air Fryer Cookbook for Beginners:

## Healthy & Easy Ninja 2-Basket Air Fryer Recipes for Your Dual Basket Air Fryer.

Helena Clark

© Copyright by Helena Clark 2024 - All rights reserved.

The content contained within this book may not be reproduced, duplicated or transmitted without direct written permission from the author or the publisher.

Under no circumstances will any blame or legal responsibility be held against the publisher, or author, for any damages, reparation, or monetary loss due to the information contained within this book. Either directly or indirectly. You are responsible for your own choices, actions, and results.

**Legal Notice:**

This book is copyright protected. This book is only for personal use. You cannot amend, distribute, sell, use, quote or paraphrase any part, or the content within this book, without the consent of the author or publisher.

**Disclaimer Notice:**

Please note the information contained within this document is for educational and entertainment purposes only. All effort has been executed to present accurate, up to date, and reliable, complete information. No warranties of any kind are declared or implied. Readers acknowledge that the author is not engaging in the rendering of legal, financial, medical or professional advice. The content within this book has been derived from various sources. Please consult a licensed professional before attempting any techniques outlined in this book.

By reading this document, the reader agrees that under no circumstances is the author responsible for any losses, direct or indirect, which are incurred as a result of the use of the information contained within this document, including, but not limited to, — errors, omissions, or inaccuracies.

# Table of Contents

## Chapter 1: Dual Zone Air Fryer .................................................................................. 8
### What is a Dual Zone Air Fryer? .................................................................................. 10
### How to Use a Dual Zone Air Fryer .............................................................................. 11

## Chapter 2: Breakfast Recipes ...................................................................................... 12
### Mushroom Omelet .................................................................................................... 13
### Breakfast Egg Casserole ........................................................................................... 13
### Banana and Raisin Muffins ....................................................................................... 14
### Smoked Salmon Scrambled Eggs .............................................................................. 14
### Blueberries Muffins ................................................................................................... 15
### Spinach Egg Scramble .............................................................................................. 15
### Cinnamon and Nutmeg Toast ................................................................................... 16
### Farro Porridge .......................................................................................................... 16
### Classic Pancakes ...................................................................................................... 17
### Matcha Pancakes ..................................................................................................... 17

## Chapter 3: Lunch Recipes ........................................................................................... 18
### Stuffed Bell Peppers .................................................................................................. 19
### Grill Cheese Sandwich .............................................................................................. 19
### Vegetable Cheesy Pizza ............................................................................................ 20
### Fresh Mix Veggies ..................................................................................................... 20
### Whole BBQ Chicken with Baked Potatoes ................................................................. 21
### Seafood Pizza ........................................................................................................... 21
### Veggie Quesadillas ................................................................................................... 22
### Chicken Sandwich .................................................................................................... 22
### Spinach-Stuffed Chicken Breast ............................................................................... 23
### Chicken Wraps ......................................................................................................... 23

## Chapter 4: Appetizers and Side Dishes ...................................................................... 24
### Sweet Potato Fries .................................................................................................... 25
### Kale Chips ................................................................................................................ 25
### Baked Potatoes ......................................................................................................... 26
### Glazed Mushrooms ................................................................................................... 26
### Classic Patties .......................................................................................................... 27
### Lamb Meatballs ........................................................................................................ 27
### Fish Sticks ................................................................................................................ 28
### Cheese Balls ............................................................................................................. 28
### Tomato Soup ............................................................................................................ 29
### Easy Popcorn ........................................................................................................... 29

## Chapter 5: Dessert Recipes ........................................................................................................... 30

- Fudge Brownies ........................................................................................................................ 31
- Pumpkin Muffins ...................................................................................................................... 31
- Chocolate Chip Muffins ............................................................................................................ 32
- Lemon Treats ............................................................................................................................ 32
- Mini Strawberry and Cream Pies .............................................................................................. 33
- Mini Blueberry Pies .................................................................................................................. 33
- Bread Pudding .......................................................................................................................... 34
- Classic Cake .............................................................................................................................. 34
- Coconut Cookies ...................................................................................................................... 35
- Chocolate Donuts ..................................................................................................................... 35

## Chapter 6: Fish and Seafood Recipes ........................................................................................... 36

- Turmeric Ginger Salmon .......................................................................................................... 37
- Salmon with Cucumber Dill Sauce ........................................................................................... 37
- Simple Salmon .......................................................................................................................... 38
- Salmon with Broccoli and Pumpkin ......................................................................................... 38
- Lemon Pepper Salmon with Asparagus .................................................................................... 39
- Salmon Bites ............................................................................................................................. 39
- Shrimp Omelet .......................................................................................................................... 40
- Smoked Salmon with Asparagus .............................................................................................. 40
- White fish with Herb Vinaigrette .............................................................................................. 41
- Beer Battered Fish Fillet with Chips ......................................................................................... 41

## Chapter 7: Vegetable Recipes ....................................................................................................... 42

- Roasted Cauliflower ................................................................................................................. 43
- Zucchini with Stuffing .............................................................................................................. 43
- Kale and Spinach Chips ............................................................................................................ 44
- Lemon Garlic Zucchini ............................................................................................................. 44
- Baked Pumpkin ......................................................................................................................... 45
- Brussels sprouts ........................................................................................................................ 45
- Potato Nuggets ......................................................................................................................... 46
- Sweet Carrots chips .................................................................................................................. 46
- Stuffed Jalapeno Peppers .......................................................................................................... 47
- Beet Chips ................................................................................................................................. 47

## Chapter 8: Poultry Recipes ........................................................................................................... 48

- Cornish Hen with Baked Potatoes ............................................................................................ 49
- Cornish Hen .............................................................................................................................. 49

Chicken legs and thighs .................................................................................................... 50

Chicken and Broccoli ....................................................................................................... 50

Chicken Wings ................................................................................................................ 51

Spiced Chicken legs ........................................................................................................ 51

Baked Mustard and Balsamic Chicken ............................................................................ 52

Glazed Thighs ................................................................................................................. 52

Chicken Schnitzel ............................................................................................................ 53

Crispy Chicken Wings ..................................................................................................... 53

Sweet and Spicy Chicken ............................................................................................... 54

Hot Sauce Chicken Wings .............................................................................................. 54

Chicken Breasts .............................................................................................................. 55

Battered Chicken Wings ................................................................................................. 55

Chicken Legs .................................................................................................................. 56

Turkey Meatballs ............................................................................................................. 56

Chicken Meatballs ........................................................................................................... 57

Orange and Maple Glazed Chicken wings ..................................................................... 57

Chicken Wings with Blue Cheese and Coleslaw ............................................................ 58

Basic Chicken ................................................................................................................. 58

## Chapter 9: Meat Recipes ............................................................................................ 59

Beef and Broccoli ............................................................................................................ 60

Steak and Mashed Creamy Potatoes ............................................................................. 60

Beef Short Ribs ............................................................................................................... 61

Beef Steak ....................................................................................................................... 61

Glazed Steak ................................................................................................................... 62

BBQ Pork ......................................................................................................................... 62

Beef Burger ..................................................................................................................... 63

Pork Chops ..................................................................................................................... 63

BBQ Beef Ribs ................................................................................................................ 64

Spicy Lamb Chops .......................................................................................................... 64

Yogurt Lamb Chops ........................................................................................................ 65

Bell Peppers with Sausages ........................................................................................... 65

Garlic Herb Butter Rib Eye ............................................................................................. 66

Lamb Kabobs .................................................................................................................. 66

Sticky Sweet Lamb Ribs ................................................................................................. 67

Sweet and Savory Lamb Chops ..................................................................................... 67

T-Bone Ribs .................................................................................................................... 68

| Easy Beef Jerky | 68 |
| Beef and Vegetable Casserole | 69 |

# Conclusion ... 70
# For Your Notes ... 71

# Chapter 1: Dual Zone Air Fryer

The Dual Zone Air Fryer is an astonishing appliance that offers a remarkable cooking experience by providing two baskets that cook food to perfection and result in crispy and delicious meals. If you have an on-the-go lifestyle, then this appliance is for you.

The Dual Zone Air Fryer ensures the food is prepared with low-fat content so the recipes deliver nutrition to the body. The dual-zone air fryer is a 6 in 1 multipurpose appliance that prepares healthy meals without compromising taste, texture, and health.

The Dual Zone Air Fryer is an efficient cooking appliance that uses hot air circulation to cook food, producing crispy and crunchy meals with less than a teaspoon of oil, resulting in guilt-free indulgence with 70-80% less fat content than traditional cooking and frying methods.

Its temperature ranges from 40 to 200 degrees C. This remarkable appliance removes outer moisture from food, creating a delightful combination of crispy and juicy interiors.

For those on a budget who hesitate to spend extra money on separate appliances for dehydrating, roasting, air frying, or other functions, worry not. This cost-effective appliance performs multiple functions, providing a hands-free and odor-free cooking experience.

Along with the 100 recipes, we have added beautiful images of the recipes and snippets of nutritional information so that the overall calorie intake process stays on the right track.

# What is a Dual Zone Air Fryer?

It is one of the highly demanded and top-rated appliances that can Air Fry, Air Broil, Roast, Bake, Reheat, and dehydrate your favorite food items in significantly less time.

**Some of its basic features are as follows:**

The Dual Zone Air Fryer offers two baskets, allowing you to cook different meals simultaneously. Say yes to a hustle-free and hand-free cooking experience.

Dual Zone Technology provides the option to use the Smart Finish feature, enabling the cooking of two different foods that finish simultaneously.

Now you can enjoy versatile cooking with six programs, including Air Fry, Air Broil, Roast, Bake, Reheat, and Dehydrate.

Moreover, it offers dishwasher-safe baskets. With its 8-quart capacity, this air fryer allows you to prepare main dishes and sides simultaneously for quick family meals. It can accommodate up to 2kg of French fries or chicken wings.

It offers two baskets and separate zones with cyclonic fans and rapid heaters.

It is easy to use, and dishwasher-safe crisper plates simplify the cleaning process, ensuring convenience after every use.

Prepare 1 kg of French fries effortlessly using only a teaspoon of oil with the dual-zone Air Fryer. Its generously sized basket offers a convenient solution for preparing family meals. The dual zone Air Fryer features an intelligent button, enabling users to select any function with a single touch.

**Dual-zone Air Fryer Functions:**

**Air Fry:** You can utilize this function to prepare crunchy food with little to no oil.

**Reheat:** Now enjoy your leftover meal by reviving it using reheat functions.

**Dehydrate:** You can quickly dehydrate fruits, vegetables, and even meat.

**Air Broil:** Uses high heat from above to cook and brown the food, similar to traditional broiling but with the benefits of air circulation.

**Bake:** Use even heat distribution to cook food, typically at lower temperatures than roasting, for items like cakes, cookies, casseroles, or anything you imagine.

**Roast:** Great for roasting meats, poultry, or vegetables to achieve a delicious, evenly cooked result.

# How to Use a Dual Zone Air Fryer

Using the Dual Zone Air Fryer is as easy as a single touch of a button. First, it's essential to coat the baskets lightly with oil spray. Follow your recipe carefully, ensuring the baskets are clean. Add the food into the designated zones and choose the desired function: air fry, bake, roast, dehydrate, or MAX crisp. Adjust the cooking time and temperature using the provided operational buttons. After cooking, remove the baskets and transfer your deliciously prepared food to serving plates.

## Cleaning Of Air Fryer

Ensure the appliance cools down adequately before cleaning; disconnect the air fryer's power cord.
Confirm the appliance has thoroughly cooled.
Wipe the outer surface with a damp towel to clean it effectively.
Use a sponge to clean the inside of the air fryer.
The dishwasher can effortlessly clean the basket, crisper plate, and accessories. Afterward, remove the residual residue using a soft sponge.

## Advantages of a Dual Zone Air Fryer

- Two zones offer simultaneous cooking as it can cook two different foods simultaneously.
- Dual Zone air fryers offer Smart Finish, allowing users to synchronize the cooking times of two foods.
- It offers versatile cooking functions and helps you prepare various dishes with a single appliance.
- It offers a large capacity.
- Separate Heating Zones ensure that each basket receives consistent and customized heat, allowing for precise cooking control. This feature is particularly beneficial when preparing foods with different cooking requirements.
- The Dual Zone air fryer is easy to clean.
- It offers an odor-free cooking experience.
- It offers a hands-free cooking experience compared to conventional cooking methods.
- It is energy and time-efficient.
- It offers nutritional-rich food.

# Chapter 2: Breakfast Recipes

## Mushroom Omelet

Cooking time: 15 Minutes | Serves: 2 | Per Serving: Calories 1000, Carbs 23g, Fat 75g, Protein 20

### Ingredients:
- 4 organic eggs, beaten
- 110 grams of mushroom, chopped
- 40 grams pepper Jack cheese blend
- 2 tablespoons green bell pepper, thinly diced or sliced
- 1 green onion, chopped
- Salt, to taste
- ¼ teaspoon of cayenne pepper
- Oil spray for greasing
- 2 brown bread slices

### Directions:
- Preheat one basket of the dual-zone air fryer by selecting AIR FRY mode for 3 minutes at 160°C.
- Crack the eggs in a large bowl and add the mushrooms, cheese, green bell pepper, and onions.
- Season it with salt and cayenne pepper.
- Make a scrambled mixture.
- Take a cake pan that fits inside the dual-zone air fryer basket and grease it with oil spray.
- Pour the mixture into the cake pan.
- Place the cake pan into the preheated basket of the air fryer and set the time to 15 minutes at 160°C using the BAKE function.
- Place the bread slices in the second air fryer basket lined with parchment paper.
- Set the time to 3- 5 minutes at 175°C.
- Check the bread halfway through the cooking time to ensure even toasting.
- You can flip the bread slices if needed.
- Once the cooking cycle completes, take out the omelet and serve it with bread. Enjoy.

## Breakfast Egg Casserole

Cooking time: 10-12 Minutes | Serves: 2 | Per Serving: Calories 1220, Carbs 17g, Fat 101g, Protein 57

### Ingredients:
- 450 grams of beef sausage, grounded
- 40 grams of diced white onion
- 2 diced green and red bell peppers
- 30 grams of sliced mushrooms
- 8 whole eggs, beaten
- ¼ teaspoon of garlic salt
- 120 grams mozzarella cheese, shredded
- Oil spray for greasing

### Directions:
- Add ground sausage in a bowl, then add the diced white onions, bell peppers, sliced mushrooms, and eggs and whisk it well.
- Then season it with garlic salt.
- Preheat the one basket by selecting AIR FRY mode for 5 minutes at 160°C.
- Select START/PAUSE to begin the preheating process.
- Once preheating is done, place the mixture inside the greased pan.
- Place the pan inside the basket; remember to remove the crisper plate.
- Top the mixture with cheese.
- Close the air fryer.
- Now, turn on the dual-zone Air Fryer, select AIR FRY mode, and set the time to 10-12 minutes at 165°C.
- Once the cooking cycle completes, take out and serve the casserole.

## Banana and Raisin Muffins

Cooking time: 16 Minutes | Serves: 4 | Per Serving: Calories 730, Carbs 100g, Fat 33g, Protein 15.1g

### Ingredients:
- Salt, pinch
- 2 eggs, whisked
- 120 grams of butter, melted
- 3-4 tablespoons of almond milk
- ¼ teaspoon of vanilla extract
- 1 teaspoon of baking powder
- 240 grams of all-purpose flour
- 225 grams of mashed bananas
- 2 tablespoons of raisins

### Directions:
- Preheat both baskets of air fryer to 170°C.
- Select the START and begin the preheating process.
- Once preheating is done, press START again.
- Take about 6 large ramekins and layer them with muffin papers.
- Take a large bowl and whisk eggs in it.
- Next, add vanilla extract, almond milk, baking powder, and melted butter to the bowl.
- Whisk the ingredients well.
- In a separate mixing bowl, add the all-purpose flour and salt. Mix the dry ingredients with the wet.
- Next, pour mashed bananas and raisins into this batter.
- Once the muffin batter is ready, pour the batter into 6 ramekins and place the ramekins into both baskets of the dual-zone air fryer.
- Set the timer to 16 minutes at 170°C in AIR FRY mode.
- Let it AIR FRY for a few more minutes if it's not done. Once it is done, serve once it is cool.

## Smoked Salmon Scrambled Eggs

Cooking time: 15-20 Minutes | Serves: 4 | Per Serving: Calories 1000, Carbs 55g, Fat 85g, Protein 38g

### Ingredients:
- 4 large eggs
- 85-90 grams of smoked salmon, chopped
- 4 teaspoons coconut cream
- 1 scallion, chopped
- 1 teaspoon capers, chopped and rinsed

### Ingredients for Tomatoes:
- 4 red tomatoes
- 2 teaspoons of olive oil
- ¼ teaspoon of minced garlic
- ¼ teaspoon oregano
- Salt and pepper, to taste

### Side Serving:
- 2-4 toasted bread slices

### Directions:
- Take a mixing bowl and whisk the eggs well. Put in the chopped smoked salmon, coconut cream, chopped scallion, and rinsed capers. Mix everything well.
- Preheat the one basket of air fryer to 165°C for scramble. Preheat the other basket to 190 degrees C for the tomatoes. Grease the small pan with oil or line it with parchment paper.
- Pour the egg mixture into this small pan. Place it inside one of the air fryer baskets.
- Slice the tomatoes in half. If they are large, you can cut them into quarters.
- Combine the tomato halves with olive oil, minced garlic, dried oregano, salt, and pepper in a bowl.
- Toss to coat the tomatoes evenly. Arrange tomatoes in the second basket of the air fryer.
- Air fry tomatoes at 190°C for about 15-20 minutes, and air fry egg scramble at 165°C for 12-15 minutes.
- Once the tomatoes are done, transfer them to a serving plate. Serve the roasted tomatoes warm as a side dish with toasted bread and as a flavorful addition to scrambled eggs.

## Blueberries Muffins

Cooking time: 15-16 Minutes | Serves: 4 | Per Serving: Calories 319, Carbs 46g, Fat 20g, Protein 6g

### Ingredients:
- Salt, pinch
- 2 eggs
- 5.3 tablespoons of sugar
- 5.3 tablespoons vegetable oil
- 4 tablespoons of water
- 1 teaspoon of lemon zest
- ¼ teaspoon of vanilla extract
- ½ teaspoon of baking powder
- 120 grams of all-purpose flour
- 190 grams of blueberries

### Directions:
- Layer about 4 ramekins with muffin papers.
- Whisk the eggs with sugar, oil, water, vanilla extract, and lemon zest.
- Stir the salt, flour, and baking powder in a separate bowl.
- Add the dry ingredients to the wet ingredients.
- Now, fold in the blueberries.
- Preheat one zone of the unit by selecting AIR FRY mode for 2 minutes at 170°C.
- Now, place the ramekins inside one of the baskets of the dual-zone Air Fryer.
- Set the time to AIRFRY mode for 15 minutes at 170°C.
- Check if it is not done, and let it AIR FRY for one more minute.
- Once it is done, serve.

## Spinach Egg Scramble

Cooking time: 12 Minutes | Serves: 2 | Per Serving: Calories 358, Carbs 3.4 g, Fat 27 g, Protein 26.6g

### Ingredients:
- 2 teaspoons olive oil
- 30 grams of baby spinach
- 4 large eggs, lightly beaten
- Salt and black pepper, to taste

### Directions:
- Preheat both the baskets of the air fryer to 170°C.
- Take the separate heat-resistant dish, add baby spinach, and put it inside the air fryer basket for 2-4 minutes at 175°C.
- Crack eggs with olive oil into another heat-resistant dish.
- Add it to another air fryer basket and set it to 12 minutes at 165°C using the BAKE function.
- Once the spinach is wilted, transfer it to a bowl or plate and set it aside.
- Add scrambled eggs to the spinach bowl and mix them with wilted spinach.
- Add seasoning of salt and black pepper.
- Serve the spinach and egg scramble as a delicious breakfast.

## Cinnamon and Nutmeg Toast

Cooking time: 4 Minutes | Serves: 4 | Per Serving: Calories 900, Carbs 128 g, Fat 30 g, Protein 8.4g

**Ingredients:**
- 4 thick slices of whole wheat bread
- 1 teaspoon of cinnamon
- 2 teaspoons of brown sugar
- ½ teaspoon of nutmeg
- 1 tablespoon of white sugar
- 2 teaspoons of butter

**Toppings:**
- 2 tablespoons of cacao powder
- 2 Bananas, sliced

**Directions:**
- Preheat both the baskets of Dual-Zone Air Fryer to 200°C for a few minutes.
- Combine cinnamon, brown sugar, nutmeg, and white sugar in a medium bowl.
- Use a knife to evenly spread butter on both sides of the bread slices.
- Sprinkle the cinnamon mixture on both sides of the buttered bread slices.
- Divide the prepared bread slices inside the dual-zone air fryer baskets lined with parchment paper.
- Air fry it at 200°C for approximately 4 minutes, flipping halfway.
- Once done, carefully remove the toasted slices and enjoy with toppings.

## Farro Porridge

Cooking time: 20-25 Minutes | Serves: 2 | Per Serving: Calories 569, Carbs 78 g, Fat 19 g, Protein 22g

**Ingredients:**
- 150-200 grams cracked farro
- 250 ml of water
- A few pinches of salt

**Add-In Ingredients:**
- 2 tablespoons honey
- 120 ml soy creamer (for pouring over the top as desired)
- 60 grams of crushed raw walnuts
- 180-190 grams of mixed berries
- Dash of cinnamon

**Directions:**
- Preheat one zone of the air fryer to 175°C.
- Add the cracked farro, water, and a pinch of salt in a heat-resistant bowl and add to the air fryer basket.
- Add half of the mixed berries and crushed raw walnuts over the farro.
- Air fry it at 175°C for approximately 20-25 minutes.
- Once the farro is cooked, take it from the air fryer and stir in honey, remaining berries, soy creamer, and a dash of cinnamon.
- Mix, serve, and enjoy.

## Classic Pancakes

Cooking time: 6 Minutes | Serves: 4 | Per Serving: Calories 924, Carbs 81g, Fat 38g, Protein 6g

**Ingredients:**
- 125 grams of all-purpose flour
- 2 tablespoons sugar
- 1 teaspoon baking powder
- 1/2 teaspoon baking soda
- 1/4 teaspoon salt
- 180 ml buttermilk
- 1 large egg
- 2 tablespoons melted butter
- Cooking spray for greasing

**Directions:**
- First, preheat both air fryer baskets to 180°C for 3 minutes.
- Combine the flour, salt, sugar, baking powder, and baking soda in a mixing bowl.
- Whisk the eggs, buttermilk, and melted butter in a separate bowl.
- Combine wet ingredients with dry ones and stir until just combined.
- Do not over-mix; a few lumps are okay.
- Lightly grease both sides of the air fryer basket with cooking spray.
- Pour the portions of the pancake batter onto the preheated air fryer baskets, leaving space.
- Air fry the pancakes at 180°C for 6 minutes.
- Carefully remove the pancakes from the air fryer and serve warm with your favorite toppings.
- Repeat the steps until all the batter is consumed.

## Matcha Pancakes

Cooking time: 6 Minutes | Serves: 4 | Per Serving: Calories 370, Carbs 72 g, Fat 7 g, Protein 7g

**Ingredients:**
- 120 grams gluten-free almond flour
- 2 tablespoons matcha powder
- 1 1/2 teaspoons baking powder
- 2 large eggs (optional)
- 2 tablespoons honey
- 1-1/4 mashed ripe bananas
- 1/2 teaspoon organic vanilla extract
- 240 ml unsweetened almond milk
- Nonstick coconut oil spray

**Directions:**
- Whisk together gluten-free almond flour, matcha powder, and baking powder in a large bowl. Set it aside.
- Whisk together eggs, honey, mashed banana, vanilla extract, and almond milk in a separate bowl.
- Combine the ingredients of both bowls.
- Preheat both zones of the dual-zone air fryer to 180°C.
- Lightly coat the air fryer baskets with nonstick coconut oil spray.
- Spoon the 1/3 proportion of batter for each pancake onto the air fryer baskets. Cook two to three pancakes at a time, leaving space between them.
- Air fry at 180°C for approximately 3-6 minutes or until the edges firm up and the bottom turns golden brown.
- Flip and cook the other side for 3 more minutes.
- Serve and enjoy.

# Chapter 3: Lunch Recipes

## Stuffed Bell Peppers

Cooking time: 10 Minutes | Serves: 3 | Per Serving: Calories 692, Carbs 45 g, Fat 41 g, Protein 34g

### Ingredients:
- 6 large bell peppers
- 200 grams of cooked rice
- 400-450 grams pork sausage, crumbled
- 220-240 grams cheddar cheese

### Directions:
- Preheat one basket of the dual-zone air fryer by selecting AIR FRY mode for 5 minutes at 185°C.
- Take a large bowl and add cooked rice and crumbled sausage to it.
- Mix it well together.
- Cut the bell pepper's top green part and remove the seeds to create a cavity.
- Slice it in half.
- Fill each cavity of bell peppers with a prepared bowl mixture.
- Grease the basket of air fryer with oil spray.
- Transfer the bell peppers to the basket of the dual-zone air fryer.
- Set the time for 160°C for 6 minutes.
- Afterward, take out the basket and sprinkle cheese on top.
- Set the time at 180°C and again air fry for 4 minutes.
- Once it's done, serve.

## Grill Cheese Sandwich

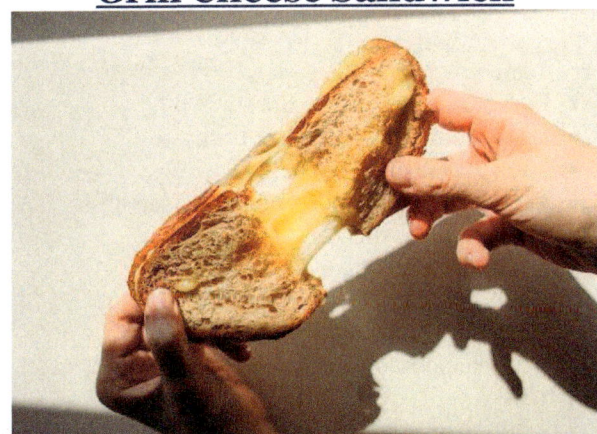

Cooking time: 10-12 Minutes | Serves: 2 | Per Serving: Calories 1176, Carbs 35 g, Fat 105.5 g, Protein 29 g

### Ingredients:
- 4 slices of white bread slices
- 2 tablespoons of butter, melted
- 2 slices of sharp cheddar
- 2 slices of Swiss cheese
- 2 slices of mozzarella cheese

### Directions:
- Preheat both baskets of the dual-zone air fryer for 2 minutes at 180°C.
- While the air fryer is preheating, brush melted butter on one side of all the bread slices.
- Add the cheddar, Swiss, and mozzarella slices on the buttered side of two bread slices (one slice per type of cheese).
- Top each bread slice with the other slice and form a sandwich.
- Once preheating is complete, open the air fryer.
- Place the prepared sandwiches into the baskets of the dual-zone air fryer.
- Set the unit to AIR FRY mode to 165°C.
- Cook them for 10-12 minutes, flipping halfway.
- Once the cooking cycle is complete, carefully remove the sandwich from the air fryer basket.
- Serve and enjoy your delicious melted cheese sandwich!

## Vegetable Cheesy Pizza

Cooking time: 6 Minutes | Serves: 4 | Per Serving: Calories 924, Carbs 81g, Fat 38g, Protein 6g

**Ingredients:**
- 1 (14-16 cm) pizza dough, whole wheat, and gluten-free
- Oil spray for greasing

**Ingredients for Topping:**
- 1 white onion, sliced
- 4 tablespoons pizza sauce
- 80 grams of mozzarella cheese
- 1/2 green pepper, chopped
- 8 pepperoni slices

**Garnish:**
- A few basil leaves

**Directions:**
- Grease one of the dual-zone air fryer baskets with oil spray.
- Flatten the pizza dough onto an oil-greased air fryer basket.
- Air fry it at 200°C for 8 minutes.
- Once the cooking cycle is complete, remove the dough and layer it with pizza sauce.
- Then, add the listed toppings.
- Add it to the air fryer basket and cook for 8 minutes at 200°C.
- Once it's done, serve with a garnish of basil leaves.

## Fresh Mix Veggies

Cooking time: 10-12 Minutes | Serves: 2 | Per Serving: Calories 541, Carbs 68, Fat 30.7 g, Protein 16g

**Ingredients:**
- 70 grams of broccoli florets
- 2-3 medium carrots, thinly sliced
- 125 grams of green beans
- 1 yellow bell pepper, cubed and seedless
- 1 red onion, sliced
- 2 tablespoons of avocado oil
- Salt, to taste
- ½ teaspoon of chili powder
- ½ teaspoon of garlic powder

**Toppings:**
- Bunch of salad leaves or spinach leaves
- 1/4 tablespoon of sesame seeds

**Directions:**
- Add all the listed veggies in a large bowl and add oil, salt, chili powder, and garlic powder.
- Toss it well.
- Now, transfer the veggies to one of the air fryer's baskets.
- Turn on the start button and set it to AIR FRY mode at 180°C for 10-12 minutes.
- Once it's done, serve with tossing of sesame seeds over a few spinach leaves.

## Whole BBQ Chicken with Baked Potatoes

Cooking time: 45 Minutes | Serves: 3 | Per Serving: Calories 1111, Carbs 18 g, Fat 118 g, Protein 4.4g

**Ingredients:**
- 0.7 kg chicken, whole
- 4 tablespoons of BBQ Dry Rub
- 4 tablespoons of olive oil
- 6-10 baby potatoes, whole and unpeeled
- Oil spray for greasing

**Directions:**
- Wash and clean the chicken thoroughly
- Remove all the giblets.
- Then pat dry the chicken.
- Coat the chicken with oil and BBQ dry rub.
- Add chicken to one of the air fryer baskets lined with parchment paper and cook for 45 minutes on ROAST mode.
- Mist potatoes with oil spray and add whole unpeeled baby potatoes to the second air fryer basket.
- To cook potatoes, select ROAST mode and set the time to 22 minutes and the temperature to 200°C.
- Flip and turn the chicken halfway through.
- Once cooked, serve and enjoy chicken with baked potatoes.

## Seafood Pizza

Cooking time: 14 Minutes | Serves: 2 | Per Serving: Calories 1594, Carbs 145 g, Fat 74.2g, Protein 85g

**Ingredients:**
- 14-16 cm pizza crust, ready-made
- Oil spray for greasing

**Topping Ingredients:**
- 4 uncooked shrimp
- 4 tablespoons of pizza sauce
- 4 tablespoons shredded mozzarella cheese
- 8 tablespoons shredded provolone cheese
- 50 grams of scallops

**Garnish:**
- 8 tablespoons chopped fresh basil leaves

**Directions:**
- Flatten the pizza dough onto an oil-greased air fryer first zone basket.
- Air fry it at 200°C for 8 minutes.
- Once the cooking cycle is complete, remove the dough and layer it with pizza sauce.
- Then, add the remaining listed toppings.
- Add it to the air fryer basket again and cook for 6 minutes at 200°C.
- Once it's done, serve with a garnish of basil leaves.

## Veggie Quesadillas

Cooking time: 8 Minutes | Serves: 2 | Per Serving: Calories 1542, Carbs 108 g, Fat 118g, Protein 26g

### Ingredients:
- 2 sliced bell peppers
- 2 onions, peeled and sliced
- 2 tablespoons of olive oil
- 4 flour tortillas
- 120 grams grated cheddar cheese
- 4-5 tablespoons sour cream for serving

### Directions:
- Toss sliced bell peppers and onions in olive oil using a large bowl.
- Preheat both the air fryer baskets to 180°C.
- Place one tortilla each into both air fryer baskets lined with parchment paper, add a layer of cheese, and top with the vegetable mixture.
- Place another tortilla on top and press it down.
- Air fry it for about 8 minutes until crispy at 180°C.
- Slice and serve with sour cream.

## Chicken Sandwich

Cooking time: 20 Minutes | Serves: 2 | Per Serving: Calories 1654, Carbs 121g, Fat 113g, Protein 50 g

### Ingredients:
- 2 chicken breast fillets
- 2 tablespoons of olive oil
- ¼ teaspoon of paprika
- ¼ teaspoon of garlic powder
- Salt and pepper, to taste
- 60 grams of breadcrumbs
- 2 bread slices

### Toppings:
- Few lettuce leaves or arugula
- A few slices of tomato
- 4 tablespoons of mayonnaise

### Directions:
- Season chicken fillets with paprika, olive oil, garlic powder, salt, and pepper.
- Then, coat the chicken fillets in breadcrumbs.
- Preheat both baskets of air fryer to 185°C.
- Add the chicken to the first air fryer basket and the buns to the other basket air fryer.
- Cook the chicken for about 20 minutes, flipping halfway through.
- Cook buns for 4 minutes, flipping halfway.
- Assemble the sandwich with lettuce, tomato, mayo, and the chicken.

## Spinach-Stuffed Chicken Breast

Cooking time: 25 Minutes | Serves: 4 | Per Serving: Calories 1042, Carbs 60 g, Fat 42 g, Protein 101g

### Ingredients:
- 2 tablespoons olive oil
- 40 grams diced red onion
- 4 cloves garlic, minced
- 60 grams of fresh spinach, chopped
- 180 grams of cooked quinoa
- 1 crumbled tofu
- 4 boneless, skinless chicken breasts
- 1 teaspoon dried oregano
- Salt and black pepper to taste

### Directions:
- Preheat both baskets of air fryer to 200°C for 3 minutes.
- Heat olive oil in a cooking pan. Sauté onions and add garlic.
- Add chopped spinach and sauté until wilted and excess liquid evaporates. Mix in cooked quinoa and crumbled tofu. Allow it to cool.
- Preheat the one zone of the air fryer to 185°C.
- Cut a pocket into each chicken breast by slicing horizontally through the side, careful not to cut all the way through. Season the chicken breasts with salt, dried oregano, and black pepper.
- Stuff the chicken breasts with the cooled spinach filling mixture.
- Use toothpicks to secure the stuffed chicken breasts closed.
- Place the stuffed chicken breasts into the air fryer baskets lined with parchment paper.
- Set it to AIRFRY mode at 205°C for 15 minutes.
- Select pause, remove the basket, and flip the chicken breast pieces after 15 minutes.
- Select air fry at 205°C for 10 more minutes. Once it's done, serve by slicing. Enjoy.

## Chicken Wraps

Cooking time: 20 Minutes | Serves: 4 | Per Serving: Calories 780, Carbs 68.7g, Fat 42 g, Protein 47g

### Ingredients:
- 500 grams of chicken breast, cut into pieces
- 150 grams of plain yogurt
- 1 tablespoon olive oil
- 1 teaspoon ground cumin
- 1 teaspoon ground coriander
- 1 teaspoon paprika
- 1 teaspoon turmeric
- Salt and pepper to taste

**For the Wraps:**
- 4 whole wheat wraps

**Toppings:**
- Greek yogurt, as needed
- Lettuce leaves, as needed
- Tomatoes slices, as needed

### Directions:
- Mix yogurt, olive oil, ground cumin, coriander, paprika, turmeric, salt, and pepper in a bowl.
- Put the chicken pieces into the marinade, ensuring they are well coated.
- Marinate it for at least 30 minutes.
- Preheat both baskets of air fryer to 200°C. Add the marinated chicken pieces into the first air fryer basket.
- Add the whole wheat wraps to the second basket.
- Air fry the chicken for approximately 15-20 minutes at 200°C, flipping halfway.
- Air fry wrap for 4 minutes at 160°C.
- Take out the cooked chicken and slice thinly.
- Prepare the wraps by placing a portion of the air-fried chicken on each.
- Add garnish of Greek yogurt, lettuce leaves, and tomato slices. Serve.

# Chapter 4: Appetizers and Side Dishes

## Sweet Potato Fries

Cooking time: 15-20 Minutes | Serves: 4 | Per Serving: Calories 1027, Carbs 100 g, Fat 109g, Protein 17 g

**Ingredients:**
- 4-6 large sweet potatoes, cut into wedges (peeled)
- 4 tablespoons olive oil
- 2 teaspoons paprika
- 1/4 teaspoon garlic powder
- 1/2 teaspoon onion powder
- 1 teaspoon cayenne pepper (optional for heat)
- Salt and black pepper, to taste

**Directions:**
- The first step is to preheat both Air fryer baskets for 5 minutes to 200°C.
- Peel the sweet potatoes, and then cut them into wedges.
- Toss the sweet potato wedges with olive oil, paprika, garlic powder, onion powder, cayenne pepper, salt, and black pepper using a bowl.
- Make sure the wedges are coated well with an even coating.
- Divide the sweet potato wedges into air fryer baskets.
- Set the timer for approximately 15-20 minutes for both the baskets.
- Shake or flip the fries halfway through the cooking time.
- Check for doneness, then serve and enjoy.

## Kale Chips

Cooking time: 9-10 Minutes | Serves: 2 | Per Serving: Calories 324, Carbs 16 g, Fat 28g, Protein 6

**Ingredients:**
- 240-280 grams fresh kale, washed and dried
- 2 tablespoons olive oil
- Salt and paprika, to taste
- 1 tablespoon of nutritional yeast

**Directions:**
- Preheat both baskets of the dual-zone air fryer to 180°C.
- Wash and pat dry the kale well with a paper towel.
- Tear the tough stems from the kale leaves and cut them into bite-sized pieces.
- Toss the kale with olive oil using a bowl.
- Make sure that each leaf is lightly coated.
- Season it with salt, paprika, and nutritional yeast.
- Divide the prepared kale between the two zones of the air fryer basket.
- BAKE the kale chips at 175°C for the first 5 minutes, then increase the temperature to 195°C and BAKE for 5 minutes.
- Once it's done, serve.

## Baked Potatoes

Cooking time: 35-40 Minutes | Serves: 4 | Per Serving: Calories 669, Carbs 72 g, Fat 40g, Protein 9g

**Ingredients:**
- 6 Russet Potatoes
- 2 tablespoons of olive oil
- Salt, to taste

**Topping Ingredients:**
- 110 grams butter
- 240 grams of vegan sour cream
- 4 teaspoons of chives

**Directions:**
- Wash and dry the potatoes.
- Take a fork and poke holes around each potato.
- Brush each potato with olive oil.
- Season all potatoes with salt.
- Add the potatoes inside both the baskets of the air fryer and BAKE for 35-40 minutes at 200°C.
- Allow the potatoes to cool once cooked.
- Then slice the potatoes lengthwise, but do not cut through.
- Take a bowl and mix all the topping ingredients.
- Top it off with the prepared mixture and serve.

## Glazed Mushrooms

Cooking time: 12 Minutes | Serves: 4 | Per Serving: Calories 677, Carbs 60 g, Fat 49g, Protein 11.5g

**Ingredients:**
- 250 grams of mushrooms, cleaned and halved
- 2 tablespoons olive oil
- 2 tablespoons balsamic vinegar
- 1 tablespoon soy sauce
- 1 tablespoon honey
- 1 teaspoon Dijon mustard
- 2 cloves garlic, minced
- Salt and pepper, to taste
- Fresh parsley, chopped (for garnish)

**Directions:**
- The first step is to preheat the air fryer to 200°C.
- Add olive oil, balsamic vinegar, soy sauce, Dijon mustard, honey, minced garlic, salt, and pepper in a bowl.
- Coat mushrooms with this mixture.
- Transfer the glazed mushrooms to one of the dual-zone air fryer baskets lined with parchment paper.
- Spread them out in a single layer for even cooking.
- Cook the mushrooms in the air fryer at 200°C for approximately 10-12 minutes, shaking the basket halfway.
- Serve with a garnish of parsley.

## Classic Patties

Cooking time: 20 Minutes | Serves: 4 | Per Serving: Calories 440, Carbs 36 g, Fat 31g, Protein 9g

**Ingredients:**
- 4 large mashed potatoes
- Salt and pepper, to taste
- 40-45 grams cooked cabbage, chopped
- 40-45 grams of corn, cooked
- 60 grams of grated cheese, as needed and optional
- 2 tablespoons of fresh coriander leaves, chopped
- Oil spray for greasing

**Directions:**
- First, season the mashed potatoes with salt and pepper.
- Mix the mashed potatoes with the chopped cooked cabbage and corn in a large bowl.
- If desired, mix in coriander and grated cheese.
- Form patties of the mixture.
- Mist the patties with oil spray.
- Preheat one basket of the Dual Zone Air Fryer to 180°C.
- Divide patties between both zones of the air fryer basket.
- Air fry them for 20 minutes at 200°C, flipping halfway.
- Remove the patties from the baskets.
- Serve and enjoy.

## Lamb Meatballs

Cooking time: 16-20 Minutes | Serves: 6 | Per Serving: Calories 1050, Carbs 73 g, Fat 31g, Protein 24g

**Ingredients:**
- 3 eggs
- 1.5 kg ground lamb meat
- 50 grams flour
- 50 grams parmesan cheese
- 1 teaspoon cumin, grounded
- 2 teaspoons onions, grounded
- 4 tablespoons parsley
- Salt and black pepper, to taste
- 125 grams mozzarella cheese, cut into tiny cubes or diced
- Olive oil spray for greasing

**Directions:**
- Add ground lamb meat, egg, flour, parmesan cheese, cumin, onion, parsley, salt, and black pepper in a large mixing bowl.
- Mix the entire ingredients well.
- Next, prepare meatballs from the mixture by placing one cube of mozzarella cheese in the middle and sealing the sides to round shapes.
- Repeat the steps until all the remaining meatballs are ready.
- Mist the meatballs with olive oil spray.
- Divide the meatballs into two baskets of the dual-zone air fryer lined with parchment paper.
- Air fry for 16-20 minutes at 200°C, and shake the baskets halfway.
- Once they're done, serve.

## Fish Sticks

*Cooking time: 15 Minutes | Serves: 4 | Per Serving: Calories 255, Carbs 18.1g, Fat 9.5 g, Protein 29g*

### Ingredients:
- 4 fillets of cod, thick stick shapes cut
- 2 eggs, well beaten
- 100 grams flour
- 1 tablespoon fish rub seasoning
- Salt and black pepper, to taste

### Directions:
- Preheat one basket of the dual-zone air fryer to 200°C for a few minutes.
- Take a large mixing bowl and add cod fish fillets.
- Whisk the egg in a separate mixing bowl.
- Combine the flour, fish rub seasoning, salt, and black pepper in the third bowl.
- Dip fish strips in egg wash, then in almond flour mixture.
- Take an air fryer basket and line it with parchment paper.
- Cook the fish sticks at 200 degrees C for the first 8 minutes to get a crispy exterior. After that, reduce the temperature to 175°C for 5 minutes.
- Then serve.

## Cheese Balls

*Cooking time: 12 Minutes | Serves: 4 | Per Serving: Calories 537, Carbs 22g, Fat 38 g, Protein 26g*

### Ingredients:
- 75 grams of feta cheese, crumbled
- 75 grams of Gouda cheese, shredded
- 50 grams flour
- 2 tablespoons mint leaves, chopped
- 1 tablespoon dried oregano
- 1 egg
- 50 grams of Parmesan cheese
- 15 grams of pork rinds, grated
- Olive oil spray for greasing

### Directions:
- Add the feta, Gouda, flour, mint, and oregano in a bowl.
- Mix it well and crack the egg into it.
- Then, incorporate all the ingredients.
- Add Parmesan cheese with grated pork rinds in a separate bowl.
- Prepare small balls of the cheese batter and roll them in the cheese and pork rinds.
- Mist the balls with olive oil spray.
- Add them to both of the air fryer baskets lined with parchment paper.
- Close the unit.
- Air fry them at 200°C for 12 minutes, shaking the basket halfway through.
- Once done, serve.

## Tomato Soup

Cooking time: 30 Minutes | Serves: 4 | Per Serving: Calories 652, Carbs 64.5 g, Fat 40 g, Protein 20g

### Ingredients:
- 1-2 tablespoons of olive oil
- 5 cloves of garlic, chopped
- Salt and black pepper, to taste
- 450 grams of tomatoes, cubed
- 950ml chicken broth
- 50 grams Parmesan cheese
- 240 ml heavy cream
- 120 ml coconut milk
- 3 basil leaves

### Directions:
- Take a heat-proof small pot or bowl that fits inside the air fryer basket.
- Add olive oil, garlic, salt, pepper, and tomatoes to the heat-proof pot and mix the ingredients.
- Put the pot inside one of the air fryer baskets and select air fry mode.
- Set the timer to 24 minutes at 200°C.
- Once done, take the pot out and blend the ingredients using an immersion blender or transfer it to a food processor to incorporate into a soupy consistency.
- Place a cooking pot over the stove and pour in the blended mixture.
- Then, add the broth, cheese, cream, and coconut milk.
- Heat it until simmering at medium to low flame.
- Top with basil and serve.

## Easy Popcorn

Cooking time: 10 Minutes | Serves: 2 | Per Serving: Calories 533, Carbs 30 g, Fat 48g, Protein 4g

### Ingredients:
- 350-400 grams of sweet corn kernels, dried
- 1 teaspoon of olive oil
- Salt, a few pinches, or to taste

### Directions:
- Preheat both baskets of the air fryer to 200°C.
- Place the popcorn kernels into a bowl and toss with olive oil and salt.
- Make two bowl shapes out of aluminum foil.
- Add kernels to the foil bowls to both the baskets of the dual-zone air fryer.
- Air fry it at 200°C for 5-6 minutes, shaking the basket halfway.
- Add un-popped kernels to the air fryer basket to let them pop again for 4-5 minutes at 200°C.
- Serve.

# Chapter 5: Dessert Recipes

## Fudge Brownies

Cooking time: 30-35 Minutes | Serves: 2 | Per Serving: Calories 1592, Carbs 186g, Fat 58g, Protein 20g

### Ingredients:
- 60 grams of all-purpose flour
- 35 grams of unsweetened cocoa powder
- 3/4 teaspoon of kosher salt
- 2-3 organic small eggs, whisked
- 2 tablespoons almond milk
- 8 tablespoons brown sugar
- 8 tablespoons white sugar
- 1 tablespoon vanilla extract
- 230 grams of chocolate chips, melted
- 8 tablespoons of unsalted butter, melted
- Oil spray for greasing

### Directions:
- Preheat one basket of the dual-zone air fryer to 160°C for 2 minutes.
- Whisk the eggs in a large bowl with almond milk, sugars, and vanilla using a hand beater.
- Put the melted butter and chocolate chips in a separate microwave-safe bowl and microwave it for 30 seconds. Once the chocolate melts, mix it well and set aside.
- Fold all the listed dry ingredients into the chocolate mixture.
- Now add the egg bowl ingredient to this batter. Mix well to form a batter.
- Spray with oil to grease a reasonable-sized round baking pan that fits in the air fryer's basket.
- Place the prepared batter into the pan, and add the crisper plate to the basket.
- Add the pan and insert it into the basket into the unit.
- Select the AIR FRY mode and adjust the temperature to 160°C for 30-35 minutes.
- Check it after 35 minutes, and if not done, cook for 5 more minutes
- Once it's cooked, take it out and let it cool completely. Slice and serve.

## Pumpkin Muffins

Cooking time: 22-25Minutes | Serves: 2-4 | Per Serving: Calories 396, Carbs 76.2 g, Fat 8.9g, Protein 8.2g

### Ingredients:
- 180 grams of all-purpose flour
- ½ teaspoon baking soda
- ½ teaspoon of baking powder
- 1 and 1/4 teaspoons cinnamon, ground
- 1/4 teaspoon ground nutmeg, grated
- 2 large eggs
- Salt, pinch
- 150 grams of granulated sugar
- 110 grams of dark brown sugar
- 360 grams of pumpkin puree
- 59-60 ml coconut milk

### Toppings:
- Icing sugar for dusting

### Directions:
- Prepare 4 to 6 cup-sized ramekins by lining them with muffin papers.
- Crack an egg and mix it well with brown sugar, baking soda, baking powder, cinnamon, nutmeg, and white sugar using a large bowl. You can use an electric hand beater to mix well.
- In a separate bowl, add salt with flour and stir. Now, add the dry ingredients to the wet ingredients.
- Gently fold in pumpkin puree and milk at this stage.
- Divide the resulting batter evenly among the ramekins.
- Adjust the ramekins into both air fryer baskets.
- Insert the baskets into the dual-zone air fryer unit.
- Set the air fryer to 200°C at AIRFRY mode and set the timer for 22-25 minutes for both baskets.
- Check for doneness; if needed, continue to AIR FRY for an additional minute.
- Remove the ramekins from the air fryer baskets.
- Serve and enjoy your delicious treats with a dusting of icing sugar.

## Chocolate Chip Muffins

Cooking time: 22-22 Minutes | Serves: 4 | Per Serving: Calories 1066, Carbs 73 g, Fat 84 g, Protein 18.6g

### Ingredients:
- 2 eggs, whisked
- 100 grams of brown sugar
- 110 grams butter, melted
- 10 tablespoons of almond milk
- ¼ teaspoon of vanilla extract
- ½ teaspoon of baking powder
- 120 grams of all-purpose flour
- 175 grams of chocolate chips
- 50 grams of cocoa powder
- Salt, pinch

### Directions:
- Prepare four cup-sized ramekins by lining them with muffin papers.
- Whisk eggs with brown sugar, butter, vanilla extract, baking powder, and almond milk in a large bowl.
- Use an electric hand beater to mix it thoroughly.
- In a separate medium-sized bowl, add flour with salt.
- Add the dry ingredients to the wet ingredients and stir well.
- Gently fold in cocoa powder and chocolate chips. Mix well to form a batter.
- Divide the resulting batter evenly among the four ramekins.
- Place the ramekins into the air fryer baskets, ensuring they fit comfortably.
- Insert the baskets into the dual-zone air fryer unit.
- Set the air fryer to 200°C on AIRFRY mode and set the timer for 20-22 minutes.
- Once done, carefully remove the ramekins from the air fryer. Let them cool.
- Serve and enjoy your delicious treats.

## Lemon Treats

Cooking time: 10 Minutes | Serves: 4 | Per Serving: Calories 702, Carbs 80 g, Fat 34.8g, Protein 21g

### Ingredients:
- 1 sheet store-bought puff pastry
- ½ teaspoon lemon zest
- 1 tablespoon of lemon juice
- 2 teaspoons brown sugar
- Salt, pinch
- 2 tablespoons Parmesan cheese, freshly grated

### Directions:
- Flatten the puff pastry dough on a clean work area.
- Combine Parmesan cheese, brown sugar, salt, lemon zest, and lemon juice in a bowl.
- Coat this mixture on both sides of the dough.
- Now, cut the pastry into 1" x 4" strips.
- Twist each of the strips.
- Transfer it to both baskets of air fryers lined with parchment paper.
- Select the air fry mode at 200°C for 10 minutes.
- Once done, serve and enjoy.

## Mini Strawberry and Cream Pies

Cooking time: 10 Minutes | Serves: 4 | Per Serving: Calories 703, Carbs 32g, Fat 59g, Protein 17.1g

### Ingredients:
- 1 Store-bought pie dough, 1 sheet
- 140-145 grams strawberries, cubed
- 4 tablespoons of cream, heavy
- 2 tablespoons of almonds
- 1 egg white for brushing

### Toppings:
- 240 grams of whipped cream
- 140-145 grams strawberries, sliced in half

### Directions:
- Begin by flattening store-bought pie dough on a clean work surface.
- Use a round cutter to create small circles from the dough.
- Brush the entire perimeter of the dough circles with egg white.
- Add a small amount of almonds, strawberries, and cream in the center of each circular dough, and cover it with another circular piece.
- Make pies from all the circles.
- Seal the edges of circles by pressing them together.
- Make a slit in the middle of the dough to allow steam to escape.
- Transfer the prepared dough into the dual-zone air fryer baskets lined with parchment paper.
- Set the air fryer to AIR FRY mode to 160°C and cook for 8-10 minutes.
- Remove the cooked pastry from the air fryer.
- Serve and enjoy by topping it with fresh whipped cream and a few strawberry slices.

## Mini Blueberry Pies

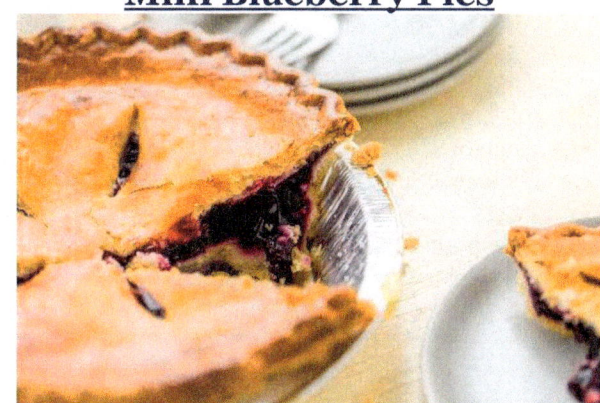

Cooking time: 10 Minutes | Serves: 4 | Per Serving: Calories 164, Carbs 23g, Fat 8g, Protein 1g

### Ingredients:
- 1 box pie dough
- 4 tablespoons blueberry jam
- 1 teaspoon of lemon zest
- 1 egg white for brushing

### Directions:
- First, flatten the pie dough onto a clean work surface.
- Cut the whole dough into small circles.
- Brush all the surface of the dough with egg white.
- Add blueberry jam and zest in the middle of each and top it with another circular.
- Press the edges and seal well.
- Make a slit in the middle of the dough.
- Add the pies to the air fryer basket using tart tins.
- Set it to AIR FRY mode at 180°C for 10 minutes.
- Once it's cooked, serve.

## Bread Pudding

Cooking time: 8-12 Minutes | Serves: 4 | Per Serving: Calories 719, Carbs 127 g, Fat 16.9 g, Protein 20g

**Ingredients:**
- Nonstick spray for greasing ramekins
- 2 slices of white bread, cubed
- 4 tablespoons of white sugar
- 5 large eggs
- 250 ml of cream
- Salt, pinch
- 1/3 teaspoon of cinnamon powder

**Directions:**
- Whisk eggs in a mixing bowl and add sugar and a pinch of salt.
- Once whisked, add cream and whisk it well again.
- Then, add the cinnamon and cubed bread pieces.
- Pour this mixture into a round baking pan, bowl, or cake pan that fits inside an air fryer basket.
- Put it inside one basket of the dual-zone air fryer and close the unit
- Set it on AIRFRY mode at 185°C for 8-12 minutes.
- Once it's cooked, serve.

## Classic Cake

Cooking time: 25-30 Minutes | Serves: 2-4 | Per Serving: Calories 1175, Carbs 276g, Fat 5.3g, Protein 8g

**Ingredients:**
- 100 grams of all-purpose flour
- Pinch of salt
- 1/2 teaspoon of baking powder
- 2 eggs
- 1 teaspoon of vanilla extract
- 10 tablespoons of white sugar

**Directions:**
- Mix all-purpose flour, salt, and baking powder in a bowl.
- Whisk eggs in a separate bowl with vanilla extract and sugar.
- Blend it well together.
- Stir the wet ingredients with the dry ones.
- Pour it into a Bundt pan lined with butter paper.
- Put the pan inside the basket.
- Now, set it to BAKE function at 140°C for 25-30 minutes.
- Once it's done, slice, serve, and enjoy.

## Coconut Cookies

Cooking time: 8 Minutes | Serves: 4 | Per Serving: Calories 288, Carbs 107.7g, Fat 8.7g, Protein 11.8 g

**Ingredients:**
- 4 egg whites
- 4 teaspoons white sugar
- 1 teaspoon vanilla essence
- Pinch of baking soda
- 80 grams of coconut flakes, shredded coconut

**Directions:**
- Preheat both the dual-zone air fryer baskets to 200°C for 5 minutes.
- Whisk egg whites, sugar, and vanilla essence in a bowl until a stiff peak forms on top.
- Now add the baking soda and coconut flakes and whisk just enough to make it a lumpy batter.
- Drop batter with a tablespoon onto both of the baskets of air fryers lined with parchment paper.
- Air fry the cookies for 8 minutes at 160°C.
- Once it's done, serve.

## Chocolate Donuts

Cooking time: 10 Minutes | Serves: 4-6 | Per Serving: Calories 835, Carbs 96g, Fat 58 g, Protein 33g

**Ingredients:**
- 100 grams of almond flour
- 50 grams sugar
- 2 teaspoons baking powder
- 2 tablespoons cocoa powder
- ½ teaspoon espresso powder
- ½ teaspoon xanthan gum

**Wet Ingredients:**
- 4 large eggs
- 60 grams of melted butter
- ½ teaspoon vanilla extract
- 2 tablespoons heavy whipping cream

**Chocolate Glaze Ingredients:**
- 160 grams of sugar-free chocolate chips
- ½ tablespoon butter

**Directions:**
- Preheat both baskets of the air fryer to around 150°C.
- Take a mixing bowl and stir together all the dry ingredients in it.
- Whisk eggs, butter, vanilla extract, and cream in a separate mixing bowl.
- Stir the wet ingredients into the dry ingredients.
- Whisk till the donut dough is ready.
- Transfer the dough into a piping bag.
- Then, fill donut molds and place them onto air fryer baskets lined with parchment papers.
- Close the unit and bake the donuts for 8-10 minutes at 150°C.
- Meanwhile, mix chocolate chips and butter in a microwave bowl; take it out once melted.
- When the donuts are cooked, glaze them with the chocolate coat. Serve once cooled off. Enjoy.

# Chapter 6: Fish and Seafood Recipes

## Turmeric Ginger Salmon

Cooking time: 9-12 Minutes | Serves: 4 | Per Serving: Calories 899, Carbs 76g, Fat 59g, Protein 31 g

### Ingredients:
- 4 salmon fillets
- 2 tablespoons olive oil
- 1.5 teaspoons ground turmeric
- 1 teaspoon ground ginger
- 1 teaspoon garlic powder
- Salt and black pepper, to taste

### Directions:
- Preheat both the baskets of the air fryer to 200°C.
- Mix ground turmeric, salt, pepper, ginger, and garlic powder in a small bowl.
- Coat the salmon with oil.
- Then, coat the fillets with the spice mixture.
- Place the seasoned salmon fillets in the air fryer baskets in a single layer.
- BAKE the Salmon in the air fryer at 200°C for 9-12 minutes, depending on the thickness of the fillets.
- Remove the salmon from the air fryer once the salmon is cooked.
- Serve and enjoy.

## Salmon with Cucumber Dill Sauce

Cooking time: 10-12 Minutes | Serves: 2 | Per Serving: Calories 1244, Carbs 116 g, Fat 78 g, Protein 58g

### Ingredients:
- 2 salmon fillets (180-200 grams each)
- 1 tablespoon olive oil
- Salt and pepper to taste

**For the Cucumber Dill Yogurt Sauce:**
- 250 grams Greek yogurt (full-fat or low-fat)
- 240 grams of cream cheese
- ½ cucumber peeled, seeded, and fincly grated
- 2 tablespoons fresh dill, chopped
- 1 clove garlic, minced
- 1 tablespoon lemon juice
- Salt and pepper to taste

**Sides:**
- 1 zucchini, sliced
- 1 yellow bell pepper, cubed
- 1 red bell pepper, cubed

### Directions:
- First, prepare the cucumber dill yogurt sauce in a bowl by combining Greek yogurt, cream cheese, grated cucumber, chopped dill, minced garlic, and lemon juice. Add salt and pepper.
- Cover the bowl and refrigerate it for a few minutes.
- Set one zone to 180°C for the salmon and another for veggies at 170°C.
- Pour olive oil over the salmon fillets and season with salt and pepper.
- Cook the salmon in the air fryer at 180°C for 12 minutes or until cooked. Adjust the time based on the thickness of the fillets.
- Add zucchini and bell pepper to the preheated second basket in a single layer.
- Air fry for 5 minutes until the vegetables are slightly tender.
- Plate the salmon fillets, top with a dollop of cucumber dill yogurt sauce, and serve with zucchini and bell pepper.

## Simple Salmon

Cooking time: 14-16 Minutes | Serves: 2-4 | Per Serving: Calories 340, Carbs 2.3g, Fat 29 g, Protein 20g

**Ingredients:**
- 4 salmon fillets, 225 grams each
- 2 tablespoons of Cajun seasoning
- 2 tablespoons of jerk seasoning
- 1 lemon, juice only
- Olive oil spray for greasing

**Directions:**
- First, coat the fillets with lemon juice and let it sit for 10 minutes.
- Now rub half the salmon fillet with Cajun seasoning and mist it with oil spray.
- Rub the remaining fillet with jerk seasoning and mist with oil spray.
- Now divide the salmon fillets between both air fryer baskets.
- Set the baskets to 190°C for 14-16 minutes on AIR FRY mode.
- Hit the start button to start cooking.
- Once the cooking is done, serve the fish fillets with a bowl of fresh salad or as per liking.

## Salmon with Broccoli and Pumpkin

Cooking time: 9-10 Minutes | Serves: 2-3 | Per Serving: Calories 868, Carbs 33 g, Fat 78g, Protein 19g

**Ingredients:**
- 150 grams of broccoli
- 200 grams pumpkin, cubed and peeled
- 110 grams of butter, melted
- Salt and black pepper, to taste
- Oil spray for greasing
- 0.4 kg of salmon, fillets

**Side serving:**
- 2 tablespoons of pesto sauce

**Directions:**
- Add broccoli and pumpkin cubes to a bowl and toss them with salt, pepper, and oil spray.
- Put the broccoli and pumpkin cubes in one basket of the air fryer.
- Rub the salmon fillets with salt, black pepper, and butter.
- Put fish inside the second basket of air fryer lined with parchment paper.
- Then, insert the baskets into the unit.
- Set it to air fry mode for 9-10 minutes at 200°C for salmon and 6 minutes at 200°C for the veggies basket.
- Hit start to start the cooking.
- Once done, serve by placing it on serving plates.
- Put the pesto aside or on top of the salmon; enjoy.

## Lemon Pepper Salmon with Asparagus

Cooking time: 12 Minutes | Serves: 2 | Per Serving: Calories 1530, Carbs 44g, Fat104g, Protein 125g

### Ingredients:
- 175 grams of green asparagus
- 2 tablespoons of butter, melted
- 2 fillets of salmon, a total of 340 grams
- Salt and black pepper, to taste
- ¼ teaspoon of paprika
- 1 teaspoon of lemon juice
- ½ teaspoon of lemon zest
- Oil spray for greasing

### Directions:
- Prepare the asparagus by rinsing and trimming them.
- Combine butter, lemon juice, lemon zest, salt, paprika, and black pepper in a bowl.
- Brush the salmon fillets with the prepared rub.
- Add asparagus to one basket of the air fryer lined with parchment paper.
- Add salmon to the other air fryer basket lined with parchment paper.
- Set the salmon basket to 190°C for 12 minutes and the asparagus basket to 6 minutes at 160°C.
- Once the entire cooking cycle is complete, serve the deliciously cooked dish and savor the flavors.

## Salmon Bites

Cooking time: 12-14 Minutes | Serves: 4 | Per Serving: Calories 1903, Carbs 121 g, Fat 130 g, Protein 90g

### Ingredients:
- 340 grams of skinless salmon fillet, cut into small proportions
- 1 inch ginger, grated
- 4 cloves garlic, grated
- 1/4 teaspoon coarse sea salt
- 1 teaspoon ground cumin
- 1 teaspoon ground coriander
- 2 teaspoons white pepper
- 1 teaspoon turmeric
- 1 teaspoon lime juice
- 2 tablespoons olive oil
- 6 tablespoons of coconut milk

### Directions:
- Take a high-speed blender and add ginger and garlic.
- Then add salt, cumin, coriander, white pepper, turmeric, lime juice, and olive oil.
- Make a smooth paste and add coconut milk to it.
- Add the salmon to the prepared mixture and allow it to marinate for at least 20 minutes.
- Add the salmon pieces inside one of the baskets of the air fryer lined with parchment paper.
- Set it to 12-14 minutes at 190°C on AIR FRY mode.
- Once done, serve the fillets and enjoy.

## Shrimp Omelet

Cooking time: 14 Minutes | Serves: 3-4 | Per Serving: Calories 857, Carbs 37 g, Fat 56 g, Protein 60 g

### Ingredients:
- 6 large shrimp, shells removed and chopped
- 6 eggs, beaten
- ½ tablespoon of butter, melted
- 2 tablespoons green onions, sliced
- 20 grams of mushrooms, chopped
- 1 pinch paprika
- Salt and black pepper, to taste
- Oil spray for greasing

### Directions:
- In a mixing bowl, whisk the eggs and add chopped shrimp, butter, green onions, mushrooms, paprika, salt, and black pepper.
- Grease a cake pan that fits inside the air fryer basket with oil spray.
- Pour the egg mixture into the greased cake pan and add it inside the air fryer basket.
- Press the BAKE function and set the temperature to 160°C for 14 minutes.
- Once the cooking cycle is done, carefully remove the cake pan and serve the dish hot.

## Smoked Salmon with Asparagus

Cooking time: 12 Minutes | Serves: 4 | Per Serving: Calories 1581, Carbs 33 g, Fat 154g, Protein 24 g

### Ingredients:
- 900 grams of salmon fillets
- Salt, to taste
- 450 grams of asparagus
- Oil spray for greasing
- 2 tablespoons of butter

### Sauce ingredients:
- 170 grams of cream cheese
- 4 tablespoons mayonnaise
- 2 teaspoons of chives, fresh
- 1 teaspoon of lemon zest
- Salt and freshly ground black pepper to taste

### Directions:
- Combine cream cheese, chives, mayonnaise, salt, black pepper, and lemon zest in a medium mixing bowl.
- Set it aside for further use.
- Rub the salmon fillet with salt and butter.
- Add it into one basket of the dual-zone air fryer.
- Mist asparagus with oil spray.
- Add it to the other air fryer basket lined with parchment paper.
- Set the unit to AIRFRY mode at 200°C for 9-12 minutes for the salmon.
- Set the basket of asparagus to 160°C for 6 minutes.
- Flip the fillets halfway through.
- Once it's done, serve with sauce.

## White fish with Herb Vinaigrette

Cooking time: 14-16 Minutes | Serves: 3 | Per Serving: Calories 959, Carbs 156 g, Fat 38 g, Protein 40 g

### Ingredients:
- 16 tablespoons parsley leaves, chopped
- 8 tablespoons basil leaves, chopped
- 8 tablespoons mint leaves, chopped
- 4 tablespoons thyme leaves, chopped
- 1/4 teaspoon red pepper flakes
- 2 cloves of garlic
- 4-5 tablespoons of red wine vinegar
- 60 ml olive oil
- Salt, to taste

### Fish Ingredients:
- 0.6 kg white fish fillets, cod fish
- 2 tablespoons olive oil
- Salt and black pepper, to taste
- 1 teaspoon of paprika
- 1 teaspoon of Italian seasoning

### Directions:
- Take a high-speed blender and pulse all the sauce ingredients in it.
- Prepare a smooth paste.
- Rub the fish with salt, black pepper, paprika, Italian seasoning, and olive oil.
- Add the fish inside one of the baskets of the air fryer.
- Set it to 14-16 minutes at 200°C on AIR FRY mode.
- Once done, serve the fillets with the blended sauce prepared earlier.

## Beer Battered Fish Fillet with Chips

Cooking time: 24 Minutes | Serves: 2-3 | Per Serving: Calories 1033, Carbs 147 g, Fat 34 g, Protein 25 g

### Ingredients:
- 125 grams of all-purpose flour
- 4 tablespoons cornstarch
- 1 teaspoon baking soda
- 240 ml beer
- 2 eggs, beaten
- 1 teaspoon smoked paprika
- 1 teaspoon salt
- 1/4 teaspoon freshly ground black pepper
- ¼ teaspoon of cayenne pepper
- 2 cod fillets, cut into 4 pieces
- Oil spray for greasing
- 2 large potatoes, peeled and sliced thinly

### Directions:
- In a large bowl, combine flour, baking soda, corn starch, paprika, salt, pepper, and cayenne pepper.
- In a separate mixing bowl, beat eggs with the beer.
- Dip the fish fillets into the eggs, then coat them with the flour mixture.
- Line one of the baskets with parchment paper.
- Add fillets to it.
- Add chips to the second air fryer basket.
- Set the first basket to AIR FRY mode at 200°C for 12 minutes.
- Set the second basket to 200°C for 22-24 minutes.
- Shake the chips and flip the fillets halfway.
- Once cooking is done, serve the fish.
- Enjoy it hot.

# Chapter 7: Vegetable Recipes

## Roasted Cauliflower

Cooking time: 25 Minutes | Serves: 2-3 | Per Serving: Calories 145, Carbs 22g, Fat 5g, Protein 8g

### Ingredients:
- 1 large head of cauliflower, washed and dry (cut the florets thinly)
- 2 teaspoons olive oil
- Salt and ground black pepper, to taste

### Directions:
- The first step is to preheat the dual-zone air fryer both baskets to 200°C.
- Wash and cut the cauliflower into florets and put the florets in a large bowl.
- Season the cauliflower with oil, salt, and black pepper.
- Divide the cauliflower into two baskets.
- Set the timer for 25 minutes for both the zones.
- Check the progress of each batch.
- You may need to toss or shake the basket to ensure even cooking.
- Once both batches are done, serve.

## Zucchini with Stuffing

Cooking time: 30-35 Minutes | Serves: 6 | Per Serving: Calories 617, Carbs 68 g, Fat 25g, Protein 36

### Ingredients:
- 185 grams of quinoa, rinsed
- 180 grams of black olives
- 6 medium zucchinis
- 400 grams of cannellini beans, drained
- 1 white onion, chopped
- 30 grams almonds, chopped
- 4 cloves of garlic, chopped
- 4 tablespoons olive oil
- 240 ml of water
- 200 grams of Parmesan cheese for topping
- 60 grams chopped parsley, topping

### Directions:
- Start by washing the zucchini and slicing it lengthwise.
- Heat oil in a skillet, then sauté the onion in olive oil for 2 minutes. Next, add quinoa and water to the skillet, allowing it to cook for 8 minutes with the lid on.
- Add the quinoa to a large bowl and mix all other ingredients, excluding the zucchini and Parmesan cheese.
- Cut the zucchinis lengthwise and create a cavity by scooping out the seeds. Fill the zucchini cavities with the prepared bowl mixture, and generously top them with Parmesan cheese.
- Divide the filled zucchinis between both air fryer baskets.
- Choose the AIR FRY function, set the timer for 20 minutes, and adjust the temperature to 180°C.
- Once cooked, serve and savor your delicious dish with a topping of parsley.

## Kale and Spinach Chips

Cooking time: 8-10 Minutes | Serves: 2-3 | Per Serving: Calories 220, Carbs 7.5 g, Fat 17g, Protein 13g

### Ingredients:
- 45 grams of spinach, torn in pieces and stems removed
- 70 grams of kale, torn in pieces, stems removed
- 2 tablespoons of olive oil
- Sea salt, to taste
- 50 grams of Parmesan cheese, grated

### Directions:
- Take a mixing bowl and add spinach to it.
- Take a separate mixing bowl and add kale to it.
- Next, season both of them with olive oil and sea salt.
- Add kale to one basket of air fryers and spinach to the second basket.
- Select the Max Crisp mode at 170°C for 8-10 minutes for both.
- Once done, take out the crispy chips and sprinkle with Parmesan cheese.
- Serve.

## Lemon Garlic Zucchini

Cooking time: 8-12 Minutes | Serves: 3 | Per Serving: Calories 28, Carbs 6g, Fat 0g, Protein 2g

### Ingredients:
- 2 zucchinis, sliced thinly
- 2 teaspoons garlic, minced
- ½ teaspoon garlic powder
- ½ teaspoon salt
- ¼ teaspoon pepper
- 2 tablespoons lemon juice

### Directions:
- Preheat both of the air fryers to 200°C.
- Slice the zucchini into round cuts.
- Add them into a zip-lock bag with all the seasoning and lemon juice.
- Shake it well and let it marinate for at least 20 minutes.
- Remove the zucchini slices from the bag and place them in a single layer in the air fryer baskets.
- Cook on MAX Crisp at 200°C for about 8-12 minutes, flipping halfway through.
- Serve once done as a side dish.

## Baked Pumpkin

Cooking time: 15 Minutes | Serves: 2 | Per Serving: Calories 412, Carbs 44g, Fat 28 g, Protein 3

### Ingredients:
- Salt, to taste
- 2 acorn squash, peeled and sliced thick
- 4 tablespoons olive oil
- 1 chopped shallot

### Directions:
- Add all the listed ingredients in a bowl.
- Toss well.
- Preheat both air fryer baskets to 180°C.
- Divide the slices between the baskets.
- Select the BAKE mode.
- Set the timer to 15 minutes.
- Set the temperature to around 180°C.
- Once it's done, serve.

## Brussels sprouts

Cooking time: 12-15 Minutes | Serves: 2-3 | Per Serving: Calories 110, Carbs 20 g, Fat 2g, Protein 5g

### Ingredients:
- 0.45 kg Brussels sprouts
- ½ tablespoon lemon juice
- 1 tablespoon honey
- ½ tablespoon extra virgin olive oil
- 2 garlic cloves, minced
- ½ teaspoon salt

### Directions:
- Preheat both the baskets of the air fryer to 190°C.
- Prepare the Brussels sprouts by washing them and trim the ends.
- Then, cut lengthwise or leave as a whole.
- Add olive oil, lemon juice, minced garlic, honey, and salt in a bowl.
- Mix these ingredients well.
- Put the glaze all over the Brussels sprouts and toss the ingredients well.
- Divide the Brussels sprouts between two baskets of air fryer lined with parchment paper.
- ROAST them in the preheated oven for about 12-15 minutes.
- Once the Brussels sprouts are cooked, remove them from the baskets.
- Serve and enjoy.

## Potato Nuggets

Cooking time: 15 Minutes | Serves: 6 | Per Serving: Calories 114, Carbs 21 g, Fat 2g, Protein 3g

**Ingredients:**
- 400 grams of potatoes, peeled and chopped
- 1 teaspoon olive oil
- 1 clove garlic, minced
- 2-3 tablespoons Parmesan cheese
- Oil spray for greasing
- Salt and black pepper, to taste
- 120 grams of bread crumbs for coating

**Directions:**
- Boil water in a saucepan.
- Put in the chopped potatoes and cook for 30 minutes.
- Drain and pat dry the potatoes.
- Take a pan, heat oil, and add minced garlic, cooking for 2 minutes.
- Transfer the boiled potatoes to a bowl, and then add cheese, salt, and black pepper.
- Mash the potatoes thoroughly.
- Make nuggets from the mash and coat all the chunks with bread crumbs.
- Preheat both the air fryer baskets to 200°C for 5 minutes.
- Grease the air fryer baskets with oil spray.
- Put the nuggets in the air fryer baskets and AIRFRY for 15 minutes, flipping the chunks halfway through.
- Once cooked, serve them hot.

## Sweet Carrots chips

Cooking time: 20 Minutes | Serves: 2 | Per Serving: Calories 156, Carbs 31 g, Fat 3g, Protein 2g

**Ingredients:**
- 680 grams of baby carrots, sliced
- 1/2 tablespoon of melted butter
- 2 teaspoons of brown sugar
- 1 teaspoon of dried thyme
- Salt, to taste

**Directions:**
- Combine the melted butter, sugar, thyme, salt, and baby carrots in a bowl.
- Toss them well.
- Line both baskets with parchment paper.
- Divide the carrots into both baskets of the air fryer.
- Air fry them for 20 minutes at 200°C.
- Once they're done, serve.

## Stuffed Jalapeno Peppers

Cooking time: 16 Minutes | Serves: 3 | Per Serving: Calories 280, Carbs 4g, Fat 27 g, Protein 6g

**Ingredients:**
- 240 grams of cream cheese
- Salt, to taste
- 6 jalapeno peppers, sliced lengthwise

**Directions:**
- Wash and pat dry the peppers.
- Cut the jalapeno peppers lengthwise, remove all the seeds, and fill the cavities with cream cheese.
- Season them with salt.
- Put them inside one of the air fryer baskets and cook for 16 minutes at 150°C.
- Once done, serve.

## Beet Chips

Cooking time: 15 Minutes | Serves: 2 | Per Serving: Calories 75, Carbs 76 g, Fat 0g, Protein 2g

**Ingredients:**
- 340 grams of beets, peeled
- Salt, to taste
- Oil spray for greasing

**Directions:**
- Peel and cut the beets into rounds, thin cuts.
- Preheat the air fryer baskets to 200°C for 2 minutes.
- Grease both baskets with oil spray.
- Layer the sliced beets into oil-greased air fryer baskets, keeping space between them.
- Air fry beets at 200°C for 15 minutes, flipping halfway through.
- Season with salt and serve once they get crisp.

# Chapter 8: Poultry Recipes

## Cornish Hen with Baked Potatoes

Cooking time: 30-35 Minutes | Serves: 2 | Per Serving: Calories 1164, Carbs 40g, Fat 78g, Protein 68g

### Ingredients:
- Salt, to taste
- 2 large potatoes
- 1 tablespoon of avocado oil
- 0.6 kg chicken leg with thighs, skinless
- 2-3 teaspoons of poultry seasoning, dry rub

### Directions:
- Pierce the large potatoes with a fork.
- Coat the potato with avocado oil and salt.
- Add the potatoes to the first basket.
- Season the meat with poultry seasoning (dry rub) and salt.
- Mist the meat with oil spray.
- Place the chicken inside the second basket.
- Set the first basket to AIR FRY mode at 180°C for 30-35 minutes.
- Set the second basket to AIR FRY mode at 180°C for 35 minutes.
- Once cooked, turn off the air fryer and remove the potatoes and chicken from the basket.
- Serve hot and enjoy.

## Cornish Hen

Cooking time: 45 Minutes | Serves: 3 | Per Serving: Calories 308, Carbs 0g, Fat 9 g, Protein 52g

### Ingredients:
- 0.6 kg of Cornish hen
- Salt, to taste
- Black pepper, to taste
- 1 teaspoon of Paprika
- Coconut oil spray for greasing
- 2 lemons, sliced

### Directions:
- First, prepare the Cornish hen by rubbing it well with the salt, black pepper, and Paprika.
- Mist the Cornish hen with oil spray and place it inside the first air fryer basket.
- Set the time to 45 minutes at 180°C by selecting the ROAST mode.
- Once the cooking cycle is complete, transfer the Cornish hen to the serving plate.
- Serve the Cornish hen with lemon slices.

## Chicken legs and thighs

Cooking time: 30 Minutes | Serves: 2 | Per Serving: Calories 1435, Carbs 19g, Fat 72g, Protein 170g

**Ingredients:**
- 2 tablespoons of honey
- 4 tablespoons of Dijon mustard
- Salt and black pepper, to taste
- 4 tablespoons of olive oil
- 8 chicken legs and thighs

**Directions:**
- Take a bowl and combine the chicken legs and thighs with all the listed ingredients.
- Coat the chicken well and marinate it for 2 hours.
- Preheat both zones of the air fryer to 180°C for 5 minutes.
- Divide the chicken between two baskets.
- Select the ROAST function and set the time to 30 minutes at 190°C, flipping halfway.
- Once done, serve and enjoy.

## Chicken and Broccoli

Cooking time: 22-24 Minutes | Serves: 2 | Per Serving: Calories 426, Carbs 4 g, Fat 13 g, Protein 67g

**Ingredients:**
- 0.5 kg of chicken breasts, boneless and bite-size pieces
- 130 grams of broccoli
- 2 tablespoons of grape seed oil
- 1/3 teaspoon of garlic powder
- 1 teaspoon of ginger and garlic paste
- 2 teaspoons of soy sauce
- 1 tablespoon of sesame seed oil
- 2 teaspoons rice vinegar
- Salt and black pepper, to taste
- Oil spray for coating

**Directions:**
- In a small bowl, combine grape seed oil, ginger and garlic paste, sesame seeds oil, rice vinegar, and soy sauce.
- Take a large mixing bowl and mix chicken pieces with the prepared marinade.
- Let it sit for 2 hours.
- Now, slightly grease the broccoli with oil spray and sprinkle it with garlic powder, salt, and black pepper.
- Add the broccoli into the first basket and the chicken into the second basket of the air fryer, greased with oil spray.
- Set the second basket to AIR FRY mode at 180°C for 22-24 minutes for chicken breasts.
- Set the broccoli basket for 8 minutes at 180°C.
- Once cooked, take out the chicken and serve it with broccoli.

## Chicken Wings

Cooking time: 25 Minutes | Serves: 4 | Per Serving: Calories 1147, Carbs 9.5 g, Fat 43.3g, Protein 16g

**Ingredients:**
- 16 chicken wings
- 4 tablespoons of coconut amino
- 4 tablespoons of brown sugar
- 2 teaspoons of ginger paste
- ¼ teaspoon garlic, minced
- Salt and black pepper to taste
- Oil spray for greasing

**Directions:**
- Preheat both zones of the air fryer to 180°C for a few minutes.
- Coat the chicken wings with coconut amino, brown sugar, ginger, garlic, salt, and black pepper.
- Mist the wings with oil spray.
- Now, divide the chicken wings into two baskets.
- Select the AIRFRY function and set the time to 25 minutes at 190°C, flipping halfway.
- Let the cooking cycle complete for the chicken.
- Once it's done, serve and enjoy.

## Spiced Chicken legs

Cooking time: 35 Minutes | Serves: 5 | Per Serving: Calories 1091, Carbs 98.4g, Fat 53.6g, Protein 79g

**Ingredients:**
- 10 large chicken leg pieces
- 2 teaspoons of olive oil
- 2 teaspoons of chili powder
- 1 teaspoon of paprika powder
- 2 teaspoons of onion powder
- ½ teaspoon of garlic powder
- 1/4 teaspoon of cumin
- Salt and black pepper, to taste

**Directions:**
- Preheat both zones of the air fryer to 180°C for a few minutes.
- Take all the chicken leg pieces and rub them with olive oil, salt, pepper, chili powder, onion powder, cumin, garlic powder, and paprika.
- Now divide the chicken breast pieces between two baskets of the air fryer basket.
- Now, set it to AIR FRY mode at 190°C for 35 minutes.
- Once cooked, serve and enjoy.

## Baked Mustard and Balsamic Chicken

Cooking time: 25-30 Minutes | Serves: 4 | Per Serving: Calories 585, Carbs 73g, Fat 25g, Protein 30g

### Ingredients:
- 1 kg of chicken legs
- 4 tablespoons Dijon mustard
- 4 tablespoons of lemon juice
- 8 tablespoons olive oil
- ½ teaspoon of lemon zest
- 1 tablespoon of fresh rosemary
- 4 garlic cloves, minced
- Salt and pepper, to taste

### Directions:
- Preheat both baskets of the air fryer to 200°C.
- Whisk olive oil, rosemary, lemon juice, lemon zest, mustard, garlic, salt, and black pepper in a small bowl.
- Coat the chicken with this mixture.
- Grease both baskets of the air fryer with oil spray.
- Divide the marinated chicken into the baskets.
- BAKE it at 175°C for 25-30 minutes, flipping halfway through.
- Once the chicken is done, transfer it to a cool rack to let it get cool
- Then serve.

## Glazed Thighs

Cooking time: 25-35 Minutes | Serves: 2 | Per Serving: Calories 631, Carbs 6 g, Fat 48 g, Protein 41g

### Ingredients:
- 2 tablespoons of soy sauce
- Salt, to taste
- 1 teaspoon of Worcestershire sauce
- 2 teaspoons brown sugar
- 1 teaspoon of ginger paste
- 1 teaspoon of garlic, paste
- 6 chicken thighs
- 1-2 tablespoons of olive oil

### Directions:
- Preheat both zones of the air fryer to 200°C for 2 minutes.
- Combine the soy sauce, salt, Worcestershire sauce, brown sugar, ginger, olive oil, and garlic in a small bowl.
- Add the chicken thighs to this marinade and let it sit for 40 minutes.
- Divide the chicken thighs between the two air fryer baskets.
- Set it to AIR FRY mode at 190°C for 25-35 minutes.
- Once the cooking cycle completes, take it out and serve it hot.

## Chicken Schnitzel

Cooking time: 16-20 Minutes | Serves: 2 | Per Serving: Calories 1763, Carbs 104g, Fat 63g, Protein 186g

### Ingredients:
- 4-6 chicken fillets
- 120 grams Panko breadcrumbs
- 1 teaspoon herb seasoning
- 2 eggs, lightly whisked
- 40 grams of plain flour
- 2 large potatoes, thin-cut lengthwise
- Salt and black pepper, to taste
- 2 tablespoons of olive oil

### Directions:
- Add chicken fillet between two sheets of plastic wrap and use a rolling pin to pound them until thin.
- Repeat with the remaining chicken.
- In a shallow bowl, combine the Panko breadcrumbs and herb seasoning.
- Crack the eggs into a medium bowl.
- Place the flour on a plate and season it with salt and pepper.
- Coat each piece of chicken with flour, then with egg wash, and then coat it with the breadcrumb mixture.
- Allow the coated chicken to rest in the refrigerator for 30 minutes.
- Coat the chips with salt and olive oil.
- Toss them well.
- Preheat your dual-zone air fryer to 200°C.
- Arrange the chicken pieces in the first air fryer basket, ensuring they are in a single layer.
- Arrange the chips in the second air fryer basket.
- Cook the chicken for 16 minutes, taking advantage of the MAX crisp at 200°C.
- Finish chips at 180°C for 20 minutes.
- Serve the crumbed chicken schnitzels with chips.

## Crispy Chicken Wings

Cooking time: 25- Minutes | Serves: 4 | Per Serving: Calories 500, Carbs 25g, Fat 27g, Protein 65.5g

### Ingredients:
- 120 grams gluten-free almond flour
- 2 tablespoons matcha powder
- 1 1/2 teaspoons baking powder
- 2 large eggs (optional)
- 2 tablespoons honey
- 1-1/4 mashed ripe bananas
- 1/2 teaspoon organic vanilla extract
- 240 ml unsweetened almond milk
- Nonstick coconut oil spray

### Directions:
- Preheat the air fryer using the MAX Crisp function to the highest temperature available.
- Pat the chicken wings dry with paper towels.
- Combine baking powder, garlic powder, onion powder, paprika, salt, and black pepper in a bowl. Toss the wings in this mixture until evenly coated.
- Utilize the dual-zone basket by placing some wings in the first zone.
- Arrange the remaining wings in the second zone.
- AIR FRY the wings for 10-14 minutes at 200°C, flipping halfway through.
- Lower the temperature to 160°C and continue cooking for 10 minutes until they reach the desired crispiness and internal temperature.
- Serve.

## Sweet and Spicy Chicken

Cooking time: 25 Minutes | Serves: 2 | Per Serving: Calories 1219, Carbs 10 g, Fat 54 g, Protein 169

### Ingredients:
- 2 tablespoons butter, melted
- 1 tablespoon hot honey
- 1 teaspoon orange zest
- 1 teaspoon cardamom
- 1 tablespoon orange juice
- Salt and black pepper, to taste
- 8 chicken legs, wings, or thighs

### Directions:
- Prepare the glaze by combining all the glaze ingredients in a bowl.
- Coat the chicken with the glaze and allow it to marinate for 30 minutes.
- Arrange the chicken thighs in both dual-zone air fryer baskets lined with parchment paper.
- Start cooking by selecting the ROAST Mode and setting the temperature to 190°C for 25 minutes.
- Serve the dish hot and enjoy.

## Hot Sauce Chicken Wings

Cooking time: 25 Minutes | Serves: 2 | Per Serving: Calories 998, Carbs 160 g, Fat 33.4 g, Protein 52g

### Ingredients:
- 1.5 kg chicken wings, pieces
- 1 teaspoon sweet paprika
- 1 teaspoon mustard powder
- 1 tablespoon brown sugar, dark
- Salt and black pepper, to taste
- 1 teaspoon Chile powder, New Mexico
- 1 teaspoon oregano, dried
- ¼ teaspoon allspice powder, ground
- Hot sauce, as needed

### Directions:
- Mix dark brown sugar, salt, paprika, mustard powder, oregano, Chile powder, black pepper, and allspice powder in a bowl.
- Thoroughly mix the spices and rub the mixture evenly over the chicken.
- Transfer the seasoned chicken to both air fryer baskets.
- Give the chicken a light spray of oil.
- Set the cooking time to 20-25 minutes at 200°C.
- Once done, serve and enjoy by tossing in hot sauce.

## Chicken Breasts

Cooking time: 25-30 Minutes | Serves: 2 | Per Serving: Calories 558, Carbs 0 g, Fat 21g, Protein 84

**Ingredients:**
- 4 large chicken breasts
- 2 tablespoons of oil bay seasoning
- 1 tablespoon Montreal chicken seasoning
- 1 teaspoon of thyme
- 1/2 teaspoon of paprika
- Salt, to taste
- Oil spray for greasing

**Directions:**
- Coat the chicken breast pieces with all the listed seasonings and allow them to marinate for 40 minutes.
- Apply oil spray to both sides of the chicken breast pieces.
- Add the chicken breast pieces to the basket and set the AIRFRY mode to 200°C for 25 minutes.
- Pause the process, remove the basket, and flip the chicken breast pieces halfway through.
- Continue air frying at 200°C for 5-10 minutes.
- Once cooked, serve and enjoy.

## Battered Chicken Wings

Cooking time: 20 Minutes | Serves: 3 | Per Serving: Calories 1260, Carbs 26g, Fat 44g, Protein 169g

**Ingredients:**
- 120 grams chicken batter mix
- 12 chicken wings
- 2 teaspoons of smoked paprika
- 2 tablespoons of Dijon mustard
- 1 tablespoon of cayenne pepper
- 1 teaspoon of meat tenderizer, powder
- Oil spray for greasing

**Directions:**
- Wash and pat dry the chicken wings.
- Using a large bowl, marinate the wings in mustard, paprika, meat tenderizer, and cayenne pepper.
- Afterward, fold the wings into the chicken batter mix.
- Oil spray the chicken wings.
- Grease both the baskets of the air fryer with oil spray.
- Divide the wings between the baskets.
- Set it to air fry mode at 200°C for 20-24 minutes, flipping halfway.
- Press start to begin the cooking.
- Once cooked, serve and enjoy hot.

## Chicken Legs

Cooking time: 25 Minutes | Serves: 2 | Per Serving: Calories 744, Carbs 51 g, Fat 24 g, Protein 77g

### Ingredients:
- 1 teaspoon of onion powder
- 1 teaspoon of paprika powder
- 1 teaspoon of garlic powder
- Salt and black pepper, to taste
- 1 tablespoon of lemon zest
- 1 teaspoon of celery seeds
- 2 eggs, whisked
- 120 ml buttermilk
- 120 grams of corn flour
- 0.4 kg of chicken leg

### Directions:
- In a mixing bowl, combine eggs with pepper, salt, and buttermilk, whisking thoroughly. Set aside for later use.
- In a separate small bowl, mix all the spices and lemon zest.
- Dip the chicken in the egg wash and then coat it in the seasoning.
- Mist the chicken legs with oil spray and coat them with corn flour.
- Arrange the coated chicken legs in the air fryer baskets.
- Set the temperature to 200°C and the timer to 25 minutes.
- Allow the air fryer to work its magic.
- Once cooked, serve and savor your delicious dish.

## Turkey Meatballs

Cooking time: 16 Minutes | Serves: 2 | Per Serving: Calories 586, Carbs 20g, Fat 28g, Protein 70g

### Ingredients:
- 0.4 kg ground turkey
- 25 grams Panko bread crumbs
- 1 egg
- 4 tablespoons fresh parsley, chopped
- 1 tablespoon low-sodium soy sauce
- Black pepper, to taste
- Oil spray for greasing

### Directions:
- In a large mixing bowl, add all the listed ingredients.
- Mix the ingredients thoroughly and shape them into meatballs.
- Mist the meatballs with oil spray.
- Divide the meatballs in the dual-zone air fryer, grease the baskets with oil, and cook for 14-16 minutes at 160°C; flip the meatballs halfway through.
- Once the cooking is complete, transfer the meatballs to a serving bowl along with your favorite side dish.

## Chicken Meatballs

Cooking time: 14-16 Minutes | Serves: 2 | Per Serving: Calories 448, Carbs 5g, Fat 19g, Protein 70g

**Ingredients:**
- 0.4 kg ground chicken
- 1 small large egg
- 1 ½ tablespoons garlic paste
- 1 tablespoon dried oregano
- 1 teaspoon lemon zest
- 1 teaspoon dried onion powder
- ¾ teaspoon kosher salt
- ¼ teaspoons freshly ground black pepper
- Oil spray for greasing or misting

**Directions:**
- In a large mixing bowl, add all the listed ingredients.
- Mix the ingredients thoroughly and shape them into meatballs.
- Mist the meatballs with oil spray.
- Place the meatballs in the dual-zone air fryer baskets, previously greased with oil, and cook for 14-16 minutes at 160°C.
- Turn and flip the meatballs for even browning halfway through.
- Transfer the meatballs to a serving bowl or dish and enjoy.

## Orange and Maple Glazed Chicken wings

Cooking time: 15-20 Minutes | Serves: 4 | Per Serving: Calories 674, Carbs 60 g, Fat 16 g, Protein 68g

**Ingredients:**
- 4 garlic cloves, minced
- 1/2 teaspoon garlic powder
- 2 teaspoons onion powder
- ¼ teaspoon pepper
- 8 tablespoons teriyaki sauce
- 8 tablespoons maple syrup
- 8 tablespoons orange marmalade
- 0.9 kg chicken wings, bone-in

**Directions:**
- Preheat both dual-zone air fryer baskets to 200°C for a few minutes.
- Combine all the listed ingredients in a large bowl and coat the chicken wings.
- Marinate the wings in the refrigerator for 30 minutes.
- Once preheating is complete, put the wings in the air fryer baskets lined with parchment paper.
- Cook for 15-20 minutes at 200°C, remembering to flip the wings halfway through.
- Once done, serve.

## Chicken Wings with Blue Cheese and Coleslaw

Cooking time: 25 Minutes | Serves: 4 | Per Serving: Calories 920, Carbs 13 g, Fat 65 g, Protein 70g

**Ingredients:**
- 1 kg of chicken wings
- Salt and black pepper, to taste
- 2 tablespoons of butter, melted
- 1 tablespoon of olive oil
- 5.5 tablespoons hot sauce
- 16 tablespoons blue cheese dressing for serving
- 400 grams of coleslaw

**Directions:**
- Add butter, salt, pepper, hot sauce, and oil in a mixing bowl and stir well.
- Coat the wings with it.
- Arrange the wings in both air fryer baskets lined with parchment paper.
- Cook them for 25 minutes at 180°C, flipping halfway through.
- Once cooked, serve and enjoy with blue cheese and coleslaw.

## Basic Chicken

Cooking time: 22 Minutes | Serves: 2 | Per Serving: Calories 335, Carbs 62 g, Fat 2.9g, Protein 167g

**Ingredients:**
- Salt and black pepper, to taste
- 1 tablespoon olive oil
- ½ teaspoon chili powder, divided
- 2 boneless chicken breasts
- ½ teaspoon oregano
- ½ teaspoon of chipotle flakes

**Directions:**
- Combine salt, pepper, olive oil, half a teaspoon of chili powder, chipotle flakes, and oregano in a bowl.
- Rub the chicken breasts with the seasoning mixture.
- Grease one of the air fryer baskets with oil spray.
- Add the seasoned chicken to the basket and cook for 22 minutes at 200°C, flipping halfway through.
- Once done, serve.

# Chapter 9: Meat Recipes

## Beef and Broccoli

Cooking time: 12 Minutes | Serves: 2 | Per Serving: Calories 1678, Carbs 151.5g, Fat 98.7g, Protein 64g

### Ingredients:
- 20 tablespoons of teriyaki sauce, divided
- ½ tablespoon garlic powder
- 4 tablespoons of soy sauce
- 0.4 kg raw sirloin steak, sliced
- 150 grams broccoli, cut into floret
- 2 teaspoons of olive oil
- Salt and black pepper, to taste

### Sides:
- 200 grams of boiled or cooked rice
- 1 tablespoon of sesame seeds

### Directions:
- Preheat both Dual-Zone Air Fryer baskets to 180°C for 7 minutes.
- Combine teriyaki sauce, salt, garlic powder, black pepper, soy sauce, and olive oil in a zip-lock plastic bag.
- Marinate the beef in this mixture for 2 hours, then drain the meat from the marinade.
- Toss the broccoli with oil, teriyaki sauce, salt, and black pepper in a separate mixing bowl.
- Put the marinated beef into the first basket of the air fryer basket.
- Put broccoli into the second air fryer basket.
- Set the air fryer to AIRFRY mode at 180°C for 12 minutes for both.
- Press START to begin the cooking cycle and allow it to complete.
- Once done, carefully remove the beef and broccoli.
- Serve it immediately.
- Enjoy your delicious meal of cooked rice.
- Top it with sesame seeds and serve.

## Steak and Mashed Creamy Potatoes

Cooking time: 50 Minutes | Serves: 2 | Per Serving: Calories 1642, Carbs 82.3g, Fat 132.1g, Protein 42.9g

### Ingredients:
- 4 Russet potatoes, peeled and cubed
- 4 tablespoons butter, divided
- 5 tablespoons heavy cream
- 60 grams of shredded cheddar cheese
- Salt and black pepper, to taste
- 2 New York strip steak, ½ kg each
- 1 teaspoon of olive oil
- Oil spray for greasing
- 2 tablespoons of steak sauce
- Few cherry tomatoes as a side

### Directions:
- Preheat the unit for 5 minutes to 180°C.
- Rub the potatoes with salt and a small amount of olive oil, approximately one teaspoon. Next, season the steak with salt and black pepper.
- Place the russet potatoes into the first basket of the air fryer.
- Add steak to the second basket of the air fryer.
- Spray the steak with oil.
- Press START to set the potato basket to AIR FRY mode for 20-22 minutes at 190°C.
- Set steak to 12 minutes at 200°C.
- After 12 minutes, take out the steak and allow the cooking cycle to complete. Subsequently, remove the potatoes and mash them.
- Add butter, heavy cream, cheese, salt, and black pepper.
- Serve the mashed potatoes with the steak.
- Pour steak sauce over the steak.
- Enjoy hot with a garnish of cherry tomatoes.

## Beef Short Ribs

Cooking time: 45 Minutes | Serves: 4 | Per Serving: Calories 973, Carbs 106.5g, Fat 55.6g, Protein 20.5g

### Ingredients:
- 1 kg of beef short ribs bone-in and trimmed
- Salt and black pepper, to taste
- 2 tablespoons canola oil, divided
- 4 tablespoons red wine
- 3 tablespoons brown sugar
- 2 cloves garlic, peeled, minced

### Directions:
- Preheat the air fryer in both baskets for 5 minutes at 165°C.
- Meanwhile, season the ribs with brown sugar, wine, garlic, salt, and black pepper, and rub a small amount of canola oil on both sides.
- Place them in the oil-greased basket of the air fryer.
- Set the basket time to 45 minutes at 200°C in AIR FRY mode.
- Press START to begin the cooking cycle.
- Once the cooking is complete, carefully remove the ribs.
- Serve the short ribs hot.

## Beef Steak

Cooking time: 22-25 Minutes | Serves: 2 | Per Serving: Calories 893, Carbs 0g, Fat 96.5g, Protein 15.2g

### Ingredients:
- 2 teaspoons of olive oil
- 1 tablespoon of steak seasoning
- 0.5 kg of beef steak

### Directions:
- Season the steak on both sides with olive oil, and then rub the seasoning all over.
- Put the steak in one of the baskets of the air fryer and set it to AIR FRY mode at 200°C for 22-25 minutes.
- After 7 minutes, flip the steak and cover it with foil on top.
- Once done, serve the medium-rare steak and enjoy it after letting it rest for 10 minutes.
- Slice, serve, and enjoy.

## Glazed Steak

Cooking time: 14 Minutes | Serves: 2 | Per Serving: Calories 2494, Carbs 216.5g, Fat 165.3g, Protein 65.6g

### Ingredients:
- 2 beef steaks (150 grams each)
- 8 tablespoons soy sauce
- Salt and black pepper, to taste
- 3 tablespoons of vegetable oil
- 2 teaspoons of grated ginger
- 6 cloves garlic, minced
- 4 tablespoons brown sugar

### Directions:
- Whisk together soy sauce, salt, pepper, vegetable oil, garlic, brown sugar, and ginger in a large mixing bowl.
- Rub the steak with this marinade and let it sit for 60 minutes.
- After the marinating time, divide the steak into both zones of the air fryer basket and set it to AIR FRY mode at 200°C for 6-7 minutes per side for medium well.
- Once done, serve and enjoy.

## BBQ Pork

Cooking time: 25 Minutes | Serves: 4 | Per Serving: Calories 239, Carbs 44.2g, Fat 1.2g, Protein 13g

### Ingredients:
- 4 tablespoons of soy sauce
- 60 ml red wine
- 2 tablespoons of oyster sauce
- 60 ml honey
- 4 tablespoons brown sugar
- Pinch of salt
- Pinch of black pepper
- 1 teaspoon of ginger garlic, paste
- 1 teaspoon of five-spice powder
- 1 kg of pork shoulder, sliced

### Directions:
- Combine all the ingredients listed under the sauce ingredients in a mixing bowl. Transfer half the mixture to a saucepan and allow it to simmer for 10 minutes. Set the sauce aside.
- Marinate the pork in the sauce for 2 hours.
- Afterward, place the pork slices in the dual-zone air fryer basket and set it to AIRFRY mode at 200°C for 25 minutes.
- If it is not done according to preference, add a few more minutes to the cooking time.
- Once done, remove the pork from the air fryer and serve it with the leftover prepared sauce.
- Serve by slicing.

## Beef Burger

Cooking time: 12 Minutes | Serves: 2 | Per Serving: Calories 1428, Carbs 103.2g, Fat 96.1g, Protein 54.1g

**Ingredients:**
- 0.5 kg of ground beef
- Salt and pepper, to taste
- ½ teaspoon of red chili powder
- ¼ teaspoon of coriander powder
- 2 tablespoons of chopped onion
- 1 green chili, chopped
- Oil spray for greasing
- 2 burger buns, toasted

**Toppings:**
- 4 cheese slices
- 4 tomatoes slices
- A few lettuce leaves.

**Directions:**
- Grease both of the air fryer baskets with oil spray.
- Add the buns for toasting in the first basket of the air fryer.
- In a mixing bowl, combine minced beef with salt, pepper, chili powder, coriander powder, green chili, and chopped onion.
- Thoroughly mix the ingredients and shape the mixture into two burger patties using wet hands.
- Arrange the burger patties inside the dual-zone air fryer's second basket.
- Set the cooking time for 4 minutes using the AIR FRY mode at 170°C for the buns.
- Set the cooking time for 12 minutes using the AIR FRY mode at 200°C for the patties basket.
- Once the initial cooking time is complete, carefully remove the basket from both zones. Remember to flip the patties halfway through cooking.
- Once done, serve the patties on the buns, making burgers and topping them with the listed toppings.
- Enjoy.

## Pork Chops

Cooking time: 22 Minutes | Serves: 2 | Per Serving: Calories 2696, Carbs 132.9g, Fat 205.5g, Protein 108.7g

**Ingredients:**
- 1 tablespoon of rosemary, chopped
- Salt and black pepper, to taste
- 2 garlic cloves
- ¼ teaspoon ginger
- 2 tablespoons of olive oil
- 8 pork chops

**Directions:**
- Mix rosemary, salt, pepper, garlic cloves, ginger, and olive oil in a blender.
- Rub this marinade over pork chops and let it rest for a few hours.
- Then, place the chops inside the air fryer and set it to AIR FRY mode for 22 minutes at 170°C.
- Once they're done, take them out and serve them hot.

## BBQ Beef Ribs

Cooking time: 18 Minutes | Serves:6 | Per Serving: Calories 289, Carbs 26g, Fat 4.1g, Protein 8.8g

### Ingredients:
- 4 tablespoons of barbecue spice rub
- 1 tablespoon kosher salt and black pepper
- 3 tablespoons brown sugar
- 1 kg of beef back ribs
- 240 ml barbecue sauce

### Directions:
- Mix salt, pepper, brown sugar, and BBQ spice rub in a small bowl.
- Grease the ribs with oil spray from both sides and then rub it with a spice mixture.
- Add the ribs inside both Air fryer baskets, and set it to AIR FRY MODE at 180°C for 18 minutes.
- Let the air fryer cook the ribs.
- Once done, serve with an additional coating of BBQ sauce.
- Enjoy hot.

## Spicy Lamb Chops

Cooking time: 15 Minutes | Serves: 4 | Per Serving: Calories840, Carbs 56.4g, Fat 30.1g, Protein 95.9g

### Ingredients:
- 12 lamb chops, bone-in
- Salt and black pepper, to taste
- ½ teaspoon of lemon zest
- 1 tablespoon of lemon juice
- 1 teaspoon of paprika
- 1 teaspoon of garlic powder
- ½ teaspoon of Italian seasoning
- ¼ teaspoon of onion powder

### Directions:
- Preheat the dual-zone air fryer by selecting AIR FRY mode for 2 minutes at 160°C.
- Press START/PAUSE to initiate the preheating process.
- Place the lamb chops in a bowl and sprinkle salt, garlic powder, Italian seasoning, onion powder, black pepper, lemon zest, lemon juice, and paprika.
- Rub the chops well and divide them into both baskets of the dual-zone air fryer.
- Air fry them at 200°C for 15 minutes.
- After 10 minutes, take them out of the basket and flip the chops.
- Continue cooking for the remaining minutes, then serve and enjoy.

## Yogurt Lamb Chops

Cooking time: 22 Minutes | Serves: 2 | Per Serving: Calories 2165, Carbs 47.6g, Fat 156.3g, Protein 154.8g

### Ingredients:
- 360 grams of plain Greek yogurt
- 1 lemon, juice only
- 1 teaspoon ground cumin
- 1 teaspoon ground coriander
- ¾ teaspoon ground turmeric
- ¼ teaspoon ground allspice
- 10 rib lamb chops ( thick cut)
- 2 tablespoons olive oil, divided

### Directions:
- First, preheat both air fryer baskets to 180°C for 3 minutes.
- Combine the flour, salt, sugar, baking powder, and baking soda in a mixing bowl.
- Whisk the eggs, buttermilk, and melted butter in a separate bowl.
- Combine wet ingredients with dry ones and stir until just combined.
- Do not over-mix; a few lumps are okay.
- Lightly grease both sides of the air fryer basket with cooking spray.
- Pour the portions of the pancake batter onto the preheated air fryer baskets, leaving space.
- Air fry the pancakes at 180°C for 6 minutes.
- Carefully remove the pancakes from the air fryer and serve warm with your favorite toppings.
- Repeat the steps until all the batter is consumed.

## Bell Peppers with Sausages

Cooking time: 15 Minutes | Serves: 3 | Per Serving: Calories 771, Carbs 9.4g, Fat 52.8g, Protein 63.1g

### Ingredients:
- 6 beef or pork Italian sausages
- 4 red bell peppers, halved or whole
- Oil spray for greasing
- Sour cream, optional as per liking

### Directions:
- Preheat the unit by choosing the AIR FRY mode for 2 minutes at 200°C.
- Arrange bell peppers in one zone and sausages inside the second zone.
- Carefully load the baskets inside the air fryer unit.
- Set the unit to AIR FRY MODE for 15 minutes at 200°C for both baskets.
- Once the cooking is finished, serve accompanied by a dollop of sour cream. Enjoy your flavorful meal!

## Garlic Herb Butter Rib Eye

Cooking time: 12 Minutes | Serves: 2 | Per Serving: Calories 2807, Carbs 142.6g, Fat 247.6g, Protein 50.1g

### Ingredients:
- 2 rib-eye steak
- Salt and pepper, to taste
- 2 teaspoons Italian seasoning
- 4 tablespoons olive oil

### Garlic Herb Butter Ingredients:
- 8 tablespoons butter, softened
- 4 garlic cloves, minced
- ½ teaspoon fresh rosemary
- ½ teaspoon fresh thyme
- ½ teaspoon fresh parsley

### Directions:
- Before cooking, preheat the air fryer baskets to approximately 200°C.
- In a bowl, combine all the ingredients for the garlic herb butter and mix thoroughly.
- Season all sides of the steak with salt, pepper, and Italian seasoning, ensuring even coverage. Additionally, coat the steaks with olive oil.
- Once seasoned, divide the steaks between both air fryer baskets.
- Cook the steaks for about 12 minutes at 200°C, remembering to flip them halfway through to ensure even cooking.
- Once done, transfer the cooked steaks to a serving plate.
- Serve the deliciously cooked steaks with the previously prepared herb butter.

## Lamb Kabobs

Cooking time: 16 Minutes | Serves: 4 | Per Serving: Calories 402, Carbs 62.8g, Fat 12.2g, Protein 19.7g

### Ingredients:
- 2 limes, zest, and juice
- 3-4 tablespoons of olive oil
- A handful of fresh mint, chopped
- 4 large cloves garlic, minced
- 1 kg of lamb meat, boneless and cubed
- 240 grams of Greek yogurt
- Salt and black pepper, to taste

### Directions:
- Mix lime zest, juice, Greek yogurt, olive oil, mint, garlic cloves, salt, and black pepper in a large bowl.
- Marinate the lamb chops in this flavorful mixture for 2 hours.
- After marinating, skewer the cubes onto wooden skewers.
- Place the lamb kabobs inside the air fryer using both baskets.
- Cook for 16 minutes at 200°C, remembering to flip them halfway through the cooking process.
- Once the lamb kabobs are tender and perfectly cooked, remove them from the air fryer and serve. Enjoy your deliciously marinated and air-fried lamb chops!

## Sticky Sweet Lamb Ribs

Cooking time: 25 Minutes | Serves: 2 | Per Serving: Calories 3510, Carbs 125.5g, Fat 316.8g, Protein 52.7g

**Ingredients:**
- 6 short ribs
- 1 teaspoon minced garlic
- 2 tablespoons olive oil
- 2 tablespoons brown sugar
- 2 tablespoons oyster sauce
- Salt, to taste
- 2 teaspoons sesame oil

**Directions:**
- Preheat the air fryer to 200°C for 5 minutes.
- Place the beef ribs in a bowl and generously rub them with all the listed ingredients.
- Grease both air fryer baskets with oil spray and arrange the seasoned beef ribs inside.
- Cook at 170°C for 25 minutes, remembering to flip the ribs halfway through the cooking time for even doneness.
- Once the beef ribs are done cooking, transfer them to a serving plate and enjoy your deliciously air-fried meal!

## Sweet and Savory Lamb Chops

Cooking time: 25 -30 Minutes | Serves: 2 | Per Serving: Calories 1961, Carbs 145.4g, Fat 118.9g, Protein 100.2g

**Ingredients:**
- 240 grams salsa
- 80 grams chopped onions
- 10 tablespoons molasses
- 4 tablespoons lime juice
- 4 tablespoons chicken broth
- 2 garlic cloves, minced
- 4 tablespoons chopped and seeded jalapeno peppers
- 1 teaspoon brown sugar
- 6 lamb chops
- 2 teaspoons olive oil
- Salt and black pepper, to taste

**Directions:**
- Combine molasses, salsa, broth, garlic cloves, jalapeno peppers, onion, lime juice, brown sugar, and stir well in a bowl.
- Transfer the mixture to a skillet and cook until it reduces by half.
- Season the lamb chops with olive oil, salt, and pepper.
- Cook the lamb chops in both baskets of the dual-zone air fryer for 14 minutes at 200°C, flipping them halfway through the cooking time.
- Once the lamb chops are done, serve them with a drizzle of the prepared sauce.

## T-Bone Ribs

Cooking time: 22Minutes | Serves: 2 | Per Serving: Calories 2688, Carbs 356.1g, Fat 115.9g, Protein 111.9g

### Ingredients:
- 2 (0.4 kg each) T-bone beef steak

### Dry Ingredients For Rub:
- 1 ½ tablespoons ground onion
- 1 teaspoon basil
- 1 ½ teaspoons red pepper flakes
- 4 teaspoons dry mustard
- Salt and black pepper to taste
- 4 tablespoons brown sugar

### Directions:
- In a bowl, thoroughly mix all the dry ingredients.
- Use the dry rub mixture to coat the T-bone steaks evenly.
- Place the coated T-bone steaks inside both air fryer baskets.
- Select the air fry mode on the dual-zone air fryer.
- Use the timer arrows to set the cooking time to 22 minutes.
- Adjust the temperature to 200°C using the temperature arrows.
- Serve once the T-bone steaks are properly cooked, and enjoy your delicious meal!

## Easy Beef Jerky

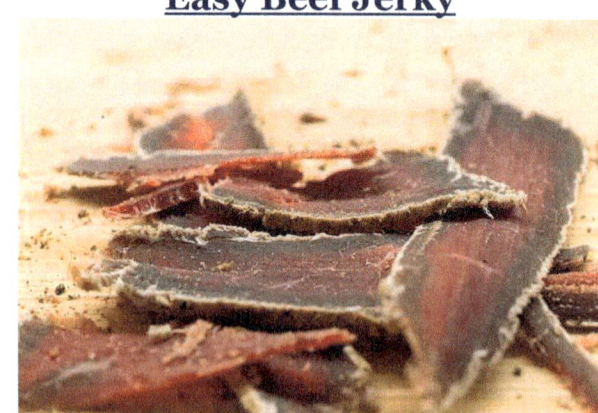

Cooking time: 4 hours | Serves:2 | Per Serving: Calories 782, Carbs 140.1g, Fat 20.6g, Protein 35.9g

### Ingredients:
- 0.5 kg flat beef, thinly sliced
- 10-14 tablespoons brown sugar
- 2 teaspoons chili powder
- 1/3 teaspoon onion powder
- 1/4 teaspoon garlic powder
- 1 tablespoon soy sauce
- 1 tablespoon Worcestershire sauce

### Directions:
- Combine all the listed ingredients in a mixing bowl.
- Place the sliced beef strips onto the cooking tray of your Air Fryer, lined with parchment paper.
- Select the dehydrate mode on the air fryer.
- Adjust the timer to 4-6 hours using the timer arrows.
- Set the temperature to 60°C using the temperature control.
- Serve the delicious homemade beef jerky once the dehydrating process is complete.
- Enjoy your homemade beef jerky as a tasty and satisfying snack!

## Beef and Vegetable Casserole

Cooking time: 25 Minutes | Serves: 2 | Per Serving: Calories 1081, Carbs 39g, Fat 87.3g, Protein 46.7g

### Ingredients:
- 0.4kg minced beef
- 5 tablespoons onion, chopped
- 8 tablespoons green bell pepper
- 120 grams of shredded Cheddar cheese
- 2 eggs, whisked
- Salt and black pepper, to taste
- 120 ml almond milk
- Oil spray for greasing

### Directions:
- Grease a round air fryer-safe dish using oil spray.
- Begin by layering half of the chopped onions, diced green pepper, minced beef, and shredded cheese in the dish.
- Repeat to create another layer.
- In a large bowl, beat the eggs and whisk in the almond milk, adding salt and black pepper to taste.
- Pour the egg mixture over the layered ingredients in the dish.
- Place the prepared casserole into the one zone of the air fryer and cook for 25 minutes at 200°C.
- Once cooked, serve this delicious minced beef and vegetable casserole from the air fryer.

# Conclusion

Preparing a crispy and low-fat meal is now effortless with this cookbook, featuring a delightful collection of the recipes designed for preparation in a Dual Zone Air Fryer.

Upon acquiring this appliance, you'll find no need for other traditional baking, roasting, rehydrating, and air frying tools. We believe you'll be amazed by its functionality, ease of operation, and convenient one-touch technology.

This cookbook furnishes all the essential information on utilizing the air fryer. Now, you can effortlessly prepare delicious homemade meals with just the touch of a button.

# For Your Notes

# For Your Notes

# For Your Notes

# For Your Notes

Printed in Great Britain
by Amazon